Rachel's Favourite Food

RACHEL ALLEN

GILL & MACMILLAN

Gill & Macmillan Ltd
Hume Avenue
Park West
Dublin 12
with associated companies throughout the world
www.gillmacmillan.ie

© 2004 Rachel Allen

ISBN-13: 978 07171 3898 2

Photographs by Suki Stuart
Food styled by Lara Stuart
Illustrations by Zink Design
Index compiled by Cover to Cover

Book design and typesetting by Anú Design
Colour reproduction by Typeform Repro, Dublin
Printed by GraphyCems Ltd., Spain

A catalogue record is available for this book from the British Library.

Contents

Great Family Meals

When the Boat Comes In

Chilli Night

Sunday Brunch

Boys' Lunch

Vegetarian Food for Everyone

Simple Comfort Food

Summer Lunch

Winter Lunch

Acknowledgments

When director and producer David Hare approached me with the idea of filming a series of cookery programmes for people like me who have a bit of a busy life, maybe juggle children and a job but like to eat good food, I immediately agreed, not really thinking anything would come of it (no offence, David!). But three or four years down the road, we finally filmed the programmes and the idea of a book came up. The original idea to do a 'tie-in' book progressed to this book, which contains the recipes from the programme and many more too. David, thank you for your vision.

While writing this book, I would quite often wake Isaac up in the middle of the night to ask him whether that recipe that I had earlier tested was really that good: thanks for your patience, Zac! Thank you to our two gorgeous little boys, Joshua and Lucca, my harshest critics who weren't afraid to say 'Yuk!' Thank you to Simone and Dodo for the constant support and inspiration.

Thank you to Darina and Tim for letting us use the Ballymaloe Cookery School to shoot the pictures for the book and for being so kind and encouraging, not to mention flexible, with my working hours for the few months while I was filming the programme and writing the book. Thank you too to all the staff at the cookery school. Darina, thank you for all the invaluable advice and for your huge wealth of knowledge, and for that I must also thank Myrtle Allen, who has always been inspiring and encouraging and who welcomed me into her family when I married her grandson! Lydia, thanks for all the babysitting!

Thank you so much to Rory O'Connell and to Diarmaid Falvey for all the good advice, and to Dervilla O'Flynn, who didn't hear about much else for ages, and to the rest of my lovely friends. Thank you Derek Tighe for saving me when I thought all had been lost on the computer and hadn't saved a thing! Thanks also to Brian Walsh in RTÉ.

So many thanks to Suki and Laragh Stuart, who are responsible for the food looking so lovely in this book. I loved working with you. Thanks to Gary O'Neill at Zink Design for his gorgeous illustrations.

At Gill & Macmillan I would like to thank Deirdre Nolan, Kristin Jensen, Michael Gill, Nicky Howard and everyone else behind the scenes for making the writing of this book such a pleasure.

Thank you Geraldine, Patrick and Mella Hare for lending us your lovely home to film the programme.

And last, but not least, I had so much fun being down in Co. Kerry filming the programmes. It would not have been possible without having such a great team – you are all fantastic: Anna Ní Mhaonaigh, Production Assistant, Billy Keady, Photography, David Hare, Producer/Director, Jimmy Connolly, Editor, Mary Harkin, Sound Recordist, Neil McLaughlan, Editor and Sally Walker, Production Manager.

This book is dedicated to Mum and Dad.
I am so lucky to have you as parents: you are the best.

Easy Entertaining

*For me, easy entertaining means casual, no-fuss cooking for
good friends. You might want to make some things in advance
or it may just be one of those impromptu evenings when you
find yourself feeding a few more people than usual!*

Herb and Fennel Seed Oil

Makes about 300 ml (10 fl oz)

Have a bowl of this in the middle of the table as an alternative to butter – fabulous to dip crusty white bread into. It keeps in the fridge for at least a month. I adore this on a cracker with soft goats' cheese for a quick snack (I'm addicted to Baking Emporium Ltd crackers, available at selected supermarkets, gourmet food shops and good health food shops).

¼ tsp freshly ground black pepper
1 red chilli, deseeded and finely chopped
3 large cloves of garlic, roughly chopped
2 spring onions (or ½ red onion), roughly chopped
3 tsp freshly ground fennel seeds
25 g (4 generous tbsp) chopped parsley
1 tbsp chopped rosemary
1 tbsp chopped marjoram or oregano
big pinch sea salt
250 ml (9 fl oz) extra virgin olive oil

Place all the ingredients except the olive oil into a food processor and whiz it up. When you have a paste, add the olive oil. Season to taste. Store in a kilner/jam jar in the fridge.

NOTE Feel free to experiment with different spices here. Ground cumin and coriander are good in this instead of the fennel, and fresh coriander too.

Breadsticks

Makes 80 small breadsticks

I love making these – they're so much better than the bought version. They also freeze very well raw, then cook them straight from the freezer. Great to serve with soups, salads, Herb and Fennel Seed Oil, pesto, hummus, a good olive oil or just on their own! This recipe makes about 80 small bread sticks, but I often make some calzones, pizzas or just plain white yeast bread with the dough too. If you just want to make breadsticks, you could halve the recipe.

For the toppings, use any of or a combination of:
sea salt
chopped rosemary or thyme
crushed cumin seeds or coriander seeds
sesame seeds, poppy seeds, pumpkin seeds
dried chilli pepper flakes
roughly ground black pepper
finely grated parmesan cheese mixed with a pinch of cayenne pepper

Preheat the oven to 220°C/425°F/gas 7. Make the pizza dough recipe from page 15 and divide it into small balls of about 15–20 g (½ - ¾ oz) each. On a clean, dry work surface (you shouldn't need any flour), using your hands, roll each ball into thin breadsticks, about 1–1½ cm (½ inch) thick. Drizzle a tablespoon or two of olive oil on the work surface and roll your breadsticks in that to 'wet' them, then roll them for a second in the chosen topping(s). Place on a baking tray brushed with water and bake for anywhere between 5 and 15 minutes, depending on how thick they are – you want them to be quite crisp and golden.

Calzones with Roast Red Onions, Gruyère and Thyme

Makes 8 calzones

A calzone is basically a pizza pie in a half-moon shape. You can also make a pizza from this recipe, but I think pizzas need to be made, cooked and eaten in quick succession! The beauty of the calzone, though, is that it can be made in advance, then just cook it when you're ready to eat. This dough is made with fast-acting yeast, which makes the whole process a lot quicker. Do make sure that if you're creating your own calzone filling that everything is cooked first, as it only heats up in the calzone.

For the calzone filling:
4 red onions, cut into quarters
3 tbsp olive oil
salt and pepper
4 tsp thyme leaves, chopped
450 g (1 lb) goats' cheese, crumbled
450 g (1 lb) grated mozzarella cheese soaked in 1 tbsp olive oil
(I recommend using a block of processed mozzarella for this, surprisingly it melts better than balls of mozzarella)
450 g (1 lb) Gruyère, grated
350 g (12 oz) sliced chorizo or any good spicy sausage (leave out for vegetarians)
20 cherry tomatoes, halved and seasoned with salt, pepper and sugar

Preheat the oven to 240°C/475°F/gas 9. Put the onion chunks into a bowl and drizzle with the olive oil, then season with salt, pepper and half the thyme leaves. Toss together and spread out on a baking tray and roast until the edges begin to brown, about 10-15 minutes. Allow to cool, then transfer to a bowl. Add the remaining ingredients, mix and season to taste.

For the pizza dough:
680 g (1 ½ lb) strong white flour
1 rounded tsp salt
1 tbsp sugar
50 g (2 oz) butter
15 g packet (2 x 7 ½ g sachets) fast-acting yeast
3 tbsp olive oil
350–400 ml (12–14 oz) lukewarm water

Place the flour, salt and sugar in a big mixing bowl. Rub in the butter, add the fast-acting yeast and mix all the ingredients together. Make a well in the centre of the dry ingredients, add the oil and most, but not all, of the warm water and mix to a loose dough. Add more water or flour, if needed. Take the dough out of the bowl and let it sit on a lightly floured worktop covered with a tea towel for 5 minutes. Then knead the dough for 10 minutes or until it feels smooth and slightly springy. You can also do this in a food mixer with the dough hook – it takes half the time. Let the dough relax for a few minutes again. Shape and measure into 8 equal balls of dough, each weighing about 140 g (5 oz). Lightly brush the balls of dough with olive oil. If you have time, cover the oiled dough with cling film and put into the fridge for 30 minutes. The dough will be easier to handle when cold, but it can also be used immediately.

On a floured work surface, roll each ball of dough out to a 30 cm (12 in) disc (if you have semolina or fine polenta, use this to dust your worktop instead of flour). Spoon one-eighth of the filling mixture over one half of the dough disc to within 2 cm (¾ in) of the edge. Brush the edge with water, fold over the rest of the dough to make a semi-circle and seal the edge by crimping with your fingers or a fork. Repeat with the rest of the dough and filling, keeping the finished ones covered while you wait. When you're ready to cook them, brush the tops with water, then slide them onto hot trays in the preheated oven. Bake for 10–15 minutes or until the calzones are deep golden brown. Take out of the oven and brush with olive oil before serving.

NOTE The water must be tepid (at blood temperature), about 38°C (100°F). If it's too hot it will kill the yeast; if it's too cold the yeast will take a long time to work.

NOTE Experiment with different fillings – it's just like making a sandwich. You can also use your favourite pizza toppings.

Gremolata Sauce for Pasta

Serves 6

A quick, simple, zesty sauce.

500 g (1 lb 2 oz) pasta
2 cloves of garlic, crushed
2 tbsp chopped parsley
1 tbsp finely grated lemon rind
3 tbsp olive oil
2 tbsp capers, roughly chopped (optional)
salt and pepper
freshly grated parmesan cheese

Cook the pasta – spaghetti is good with this. While it's cooking, mix together all the remaining ingredients for the gremolata. Drain the pasta when it's cooked, add the sauce and salt and pepper to taste. Serve with a little freshly grated parmesan cheese.

NOTE This keeps in the fridge for nearly a week and is also great drizzled over pan-fried fish or pan-fried, roast or barbequed lamb, served with new potatoes.

  Easy Entertaining

Salad of Goats' Cheese with Rocket and Honey

Serves 4

Darina and her brother, Rory O'Connell, tasted something like this in Italy, where it's quite common to drizzle your cheese with honey. This has to be the simplest but most divine salad. Assemble it at the last moment; it only takes a second. It would normally be served as a starter, but sometimes if I've been eating all day and just want something really light for supper, this is perfect.

4 handfuls rocket leaves
200 g (7 oz) soft goats' cheese (I love Ardsallagh)
4 tsp good honey
1 lemon wedge
sea salt and freshly ground black pepper
a drizzle of your best olive oil

Divide the rocket leaves between 4 plates or 1 large serving plate. Roughly break up the goats' cheese into 2 cm (¾ in) pieces and scatter on top of the leaves, then drizzle each plate with 1 tsp honey and a squeeze of lemon juice. Season with salt and pepper and finish with a drizzle of olive oil. Serve straight away.

Pasta with Spicy Sausage and Cream

Serves 6

This is a fab pasta sauce, with a bit of a kick. We make this at the cookery school quite a bit and people always love it. Just leave out the sausage for a vegetarian pasta sauce. It also freezes well.

700 g (1 lb 9 oz) fresh ripe tomatoes, peeled and roughly chopped or 2 x
400 g (14 oz) tins of tomatoes
25 g (1 oz) butter
4 cloves of garlic, grated or crushed
2 tsp chopped rosemary
salt, pepper and sugar
225 g (8 oz) chorizo or kabanossi sausage, sliced into ½ cm (¼ in) rounds
a pinch of dried chilli pepper flakes
175 ml (6 fl oz) cream
2 tbsp chopped parsley
500 g (1 lb 2 oz) penne, rigatoni, farfalle, etc.
4 tbsp grated parmesan cheese

First of all, peel your tomatoes. To do this, either boil plenty of water in the kettle or bring a pot full of water to the boil on the hob. Cut an X into the bottom of each tomato. Then, when the water is boiling, either place the tomatoes into the pot or pour the boiled water over them in a heat-proof bowl. Leave to sit for 15 seconds or until the skins have started to peel away. Drain and allow to cool. When cool enough to handle, slip the skins off and discard.

Melt the butter in a large saucepan, then add the chopped tomatoes, garlic and rosemary. Season with salt, pepper and sugar (the sugar really helps the tomatoes). Cook until the tomatoes have just begun to soften, about 5 minutes. Add the sausage to the pan with the chilli flakes, cream and half the chopped parsley. Allow to simmer with the lid off until the mixture has reduced by half, 10–20 minutes, stirring frequently. Take off the heat and taste for seasoning.

Meanwhile, cook the pasta in a large pot of salted boiling water until it's slightly al dente, then drain and toss with the sauce. Put into a big serving bowl and scatter with the grated parmesan cheese and the rest of the parsley.

NOTE If you need to cook your pasta slightly ahead of time, keep about 50 ml (2 fl oz) of the pasta cooking water in with the pasta, along with a good glug of olive oil. You can then reheat the pasta on the hob or in a microwave. Adding the cooking water and the olive oil prevents the pasta from sticking together, and using more water rather than oil keeps the pasta from becoming too oily.

Spanish Tortilla with Bacon, Gruyère and Marjoram

Serves 4

A tortilla is Spain's answer to Italy's frittata. Traditionally it has onion and potato in it, but sometimes you find meat in it too. Not only is the tortilla eaten hot out of the frying pan, but it can also be eaten cold, as a picnic or delicious on the beach at lunchtime.

This is a variation that we often have at home for totally easy, casual entertaining. Serve with a salad. Some pesto is good drizzled over this too.

3 tbsp olive oil
200 g (7 oz) bacon, cut into lardons ½ cm x 2 cm (¼ in x ¾ in) long
(I love Gubbeen bacon)
1 large onion, finely chopped
6 eggs (the better the eggs, the better the omelette)
150 ml (5 fl oz) cream
125 g (4½ oz) Gruyère cheese, grated
1 tbsp marjoram, chopped
salt and pepper
10 small or 5 medium cooked new potatoes (in winter use other potatoes), sliced 1 cm (½ in) thick

You will also need a frying pan for this.

Put a frying pan, non-stick if you like, on a high heat. When hot add the olive oil, bacon lardons and the chopped onion. Cook until the bacon is crispy and the onion is nice and golden. Take off the heat for a moment to cool down slightly.

Meanwhile, preheat the grill and whisk the eggs in a big bowl. Add the cream, grated cheese, chopped marjoram, salt and pepper to taste (I don't mind tasting the tiniest bit of raw egg for seasoning) and whisk to combine, then stir in the sliced cooked potatoes. Put the frying pan back on the heat, but turn it down to low. Add the egg mixture and cook slowly until the bottom is golden brown, then put under the hot grill for a couple of minutes, until the top is just set. Turn it out onto a plate to serve and scatter with some marjoram leaves if you like. If I'm using a nice-looking, rustic cast iron frying pan I just put the whole pan on a board on the table and serve it from there.

NOTE You could also make individual tortillas by brushing a muffin tin with olive oil and then filling each cup three-quarters full. Pop into the oven heated to 180°C/350°F/gas 4 for 20–25 minutes or until firm in the centre. Made this way, you should get 20 individual tortillas.

Parsley Pesto

Makes about 150 ml (5 fl oz)

This is a surprisingly good sauce. Sometimes I even prefer it to the classic basil pesto. Serve it as you would basil pesto: with pasta, over roasted or chargrilled vegetables, with barbequed or grilled meats, as part of a salad or on a simple crostini or bruschetta with some roast peppers and cheese. This quantity makes 1 jam jar full. To keep it at its best, store it in a sterilised jar in the fridge and always keep it covered in a layer of olive oil 1 cm (½ in) thick. Try replacing half the parsley with mint, coriander, rocket, wild garlic leaves...the possibilities are endless.

25 g (1 oz) parsley, chopped
25 g (1 oz) freshly grated parmesan cheese
25 g (1 oz) pine nuts
2 cloves of garlic, crushed
75 ml (3 fl oz) extra virgin olive oil
salt

Put all the ingredients except the olive oil into a food processor and whiz up. Add the oil and a pinch of salt and taste. Pour into a sterilised jar, cover with 1 cm (½ in) of oil and store in the fridge. Keeps for months.

  Easy Entertaining

Chocolate Mousse

Fills about 10 small glasses

120 g (4½ oz) good-quality dark chocolate
120 ml (4 fl oz) cream
1–2 tbsp rum, brandy, Grand Marnier or 1 tsp grated orange
rind (optional)
2 eggs, separated

Finely chop the chocolate. In a saucepan, bring the cream up to the boil, turn off the heat, add the chocolate to the cream and stir it around until the chocolate melts. Add the booze, if using, and whisk in the egg yolks. In a separate clean, dry bowl, whisk the egg whites until just stiff, then stir a quarter of the egg white into the cream mixture. Gently fold in the rest of the egg whites, being careful not to knock all the air out. Spoon into little bowls, glasses or cups and leave for an hour or two in the fridge to set. Serve with Coconut or Almond Macaroons (page 24) or amaretti biscuits.

NOTE You could put a macaroon into each little glass or cup and top up with the chocolate mousse. Pop into the fridge for an hour or two to set.

NOTE For a really intense chocolate mousse, leave out the two beaten egg whites and serve in tiny espresso cups.

NOTE To make chocolate mousse infused with earl grey tea, put 2 tsp earl grey tea leaves into the saucepan with the cream and bring up to the boil, then strain the leaves out of the cream and proceed as above.

Coconut or Almond Macaroons

Makes 12–16

These are so simple to make and can easily keep for 4 or 5 days in an airtight container.

110 g (4 oz) desiccated coconut or ground almonds
75 g (3 oz) caster sugar
1 egg white, lightly beaten

Preheat the oven to 180°C/350°F/gas 4. Put the desiccated coconut or ground almonds, caster sugar and the egg white into a bowl and stir to combine. It should be firm, but slightly sticky. Roll small dessertspoonfuls of the mixture into balls and place on a baking tray lined with parchment paper. Flatten slightly with a wet fork. Cook for about 10 minutes or until pale golden. Cool on a wire rack.

NOTE These are also good with the grated zest of 1 lemon or orange mixed in with the coconut/almonds and sugar.

Roast Fruit with Honey Cream

Serves 4

Peaches, nectarines, plums, bananas and berries all work well for this incredibly delicious dessert. Sometimes I use a mixture of fruit for this, sometimes I use just peaches or nectarines.

4 peaches
4 nectarines
4 plums
2 bananas
mix of berries
4 tbsp honey
cream

Preheat the oven to 230°C/450°F/gas 8. Cut the peaches, nectarines or plums in half and remove the stone, peel the banana and cut in half lengthways and leave the berries whole. Place all the fruit (cut side up) into one big or several individual gratin dishes and drizzle with honey, about 1 tbsp per portion. Put into the hot oven and cook for 10–15 minutes or until the fruit is soft and the honey and juices are bubbling. Serve with some softly whipped cream (or natural yoghurt) through which you have folded some honey, about 1 tbsp for every 250 ml (9 fl oz). Divine!

Affogato al Caffe

Serves 4

This favourite Italian dessert is not for those who are planning to go to bed as soon as dinner is finished. If you don't have the right equipment to make a proper espresso, then make some seriously good fresh coffee (see page 96). A little grated chocolate is good over these too!

4 scoops of good-quality vanilla ice cream (you could even try using chocolate ice cream, if you prefer)
4 espressos

Put a scoop of ice cream into a little coffee cup, pour over the hot espresso and serve immediately.

Summer Madness

Serves 2–4

What a great way to start a party!

50 ml (2 fl oz) sweet vermouth, such as Martini
50 ml (2 fl oz) Campari
50 ml (2 fl oz) vodka
100 ml (3½ fl oz) Cointreau
juice of 1 lime
juice of 1–2 oranges
soda water (optional)

Mix everything together and shake with some ice to chill, either stirred in a jug or shaken in a cocktail shaker, then remove the ice (if you like) to serve. Also good with a dash of soda water thrown in.

Easy Entertaining

An Indoor Picnic

This is a cross between Spanish tapas, Italian antipasti and Arabic mezze. I serve this kind of food in lots of little bowls and let everyone help themselves. The pitta crisps can be dipped into each little bowl and eaten with your hands as an appetiser or for a main course in itself with or without plates.

Lamb with Raisins and Pine Nuts

Serves 3 as a main course

This is the fastest lamb dish I know. It's excellent served with the couscous for a main course. It's also amazing in a hot pitta bread with yoghurt, Coriander and Mint Salsa (page 31) and some lettuce. Served in the pitta it would be great for a packed lunch, as it's quite dry so it won't go everywhere. Good served hot or just at room temperature.

2 tbsp sunflower oil
450 g (1 lb) shoulder of lamb with all the fat removed and cut into ½ cm (¼ inch) pieces
salt and pepper
1 level tsp ground cumin
1 level tsp ground coriander
60 g (2 oz) pine nuts, toasted in a moderate oven or on a frying pan until golden brown
2 tbsp hummus (page 31)
2 tbsp raisins
1 tbsp chopped fresh coriander

Heat the oil in a hot pan, toss in the meat and season with salt and pepper. Add the cumin and coriander and cook over a high heat for 5 minutes, then add the pine nuts, hummus, raisins and chopped coriander. Stir to mix and let simmer for 1 minute. Season to taste.

An Indoor Picnic

Couscous with Mint

Serves 6 as an accompaniment to a meal or
12 as part of an indoor picnic

250 g (9 oz) couscous
2 tbsp olive oil
300 ml (10 fl oz) boiling water, vegetable stock or chicken stock
2 tbsp chopped mint
salt and pepper

Preheat the oven to 180°C/350°F/gas 4. Put the couscous into a heat-proof bowl, pour in the olive oil and rub it into the couscous with your fingers. Stir in the water or stock and cover the bowl with tin foil or a glass plate and put into the oven for 10 minutes or until hot. Add chopped mint and season to taste.

NOTE This is also good at room temperature, in which case don't put it in the oven and just let it sit for 10 minutes on your worktop to soak up the liquid.

NOTE Couscous is a fantastic base for salads. Toasted pine nuts, feta cheese, roasted peppers, halved cherry tomatoes, Parsley Pesto (page 22) and chopped, cooked chicken work very well.

Roast Aubergine and Garlic Purée

Serves 4–6

This is a little bit like baba ghannouj, which also contains tahini paste and crushed cumin. Sometimes I put chopped parsley, mint, marjoram or coriander in too. It's also delicious spread on Garlic Crostinis (page 148).

2 medium aubergines
4–6 cloves of garlic, peeled
90 ml (3 fl oz) olive oil
juice of ½–1 lemon
salt and pepper

Cut the aubergines in half lengthwise and place skin side down on a baking tray. Drizzle with a little of the olive oil and season. Add the whole peeled cloves of garlic to the tray and bake in an oven heated at 180°C/350°F/gas 4 for 20–30 minutes or until the garlic and aubergines are soft. Using a metal spoon, scrape the flesh from the skin of the aubergines. Discard the skin and put the flesh into a food processor with the garlic, olive oil and lemon juice. Blend until smooth. Check for seasoning and serve.

Coriander and Mint Salsa

Serves 4–6

This is a pesto of sorts, so it's incredibly versatile.

4 tbsp roughly chopped fresh coriander, soft stalks included
2 tbsp roughly chopped fresh mint
2 cloves of garlic, mashed
1 spring onion, finely chopped
175 ml (6 fl oz) olive oil
salt and pepper

Whiz all the ingredients in a food processor, adding the oil after the herbs have been chopped. Check seasoning and add more oil if necessary.

Hummus

Makes 450 ml (16 fl oz)

Hummus is actually the Arabic word for chickpea.

400 g (14 oz) tin of chickpeas, drained or 200 g (7 oz) dried chickpeas,
soaked in water overnight, then drained and cooked in fresh water until
soft
2 cloves garlic, crushed
2 good tbsp of tahini (sesame seed paste)
3–4 tbsp olive oil
juice of ½–1 lemon
salt

Put all the ingredients into a food processor and pulse until smooth. Check for seasoning, then add more olive oil or some natural yoghurt if it's too thick. Keeps in the fridge for up to a week.

Butterbeans with Rosemary and Semi-Sun-Dried Tomatoes

Makes 450 ml (16 fl oz)

Another really fast little recipe, this is also wonderful served as a pasta sauce, with lots of grated parmesan. Good served with barbequed or roast lamb too.

400 g (14 oz) tin of butterbeans or any other white beans, like cannellini, or 200 g (7 oz) of dried beans, soaked in water overnight, then drained and cooked in fresh water until soft
3 tbsp olive oil
3 tbsp of chopped semi-sun-dried tomatoes – these are slightly softer and less strong than plain sun-dried tomatoes, but the plain ones will do if you can't get the other ones
1 dessertspoon of chopped rosemary
sea salt and pepper

Drain the liquid off the beans from the tin, then put the beans into a small saucepan. Heat up gently and add in the olive oil, semi-sun-dried tomatoes, chopped rosemary and some sea salt and pepper to taste. When warm put into a bowl and let the flavours infuse.

Rocket, Pear and Blue Cheese Salad

Smoked Mackerel Pâté

Pea and Coriander Soup

Breadsticks

Crema Seville

Spicy Pitta Wedges

Makes 12 wedges

These are used for dipping into and scooping up all of these little mezze/tapas dishes. I love them still slightly warm, but they're also delicious a day or two later to serve with cheese, if you have any left over!

2 oval pitta breads
a few tbsp olive oil
sea salt
2 tsp cumin seeds, toasted and crushed in a pestle and mortar

Preheat the oven to 220°C/425°F/gas 7. Cut the pitta bread into wedges or strips, put into a big bowl and toss together with enough olive oil to coat, then add the sea salt and crushed cumin. Spread out flat on a baking tray and cook in the hot oven for about 5 minutes or until pale golden. Watch out – they burn quickly!

Feta with Fennel Seeds and Olive Oil

feta
fennel seeds, ground
pepper
olive oil

Crumble up some feta cheese into 2 cm (¾ in) chunks. Add some freshly ground fennel seeds, black pepper and drizzle with olive oil.

I also like to serve this with some caper berries, slices of prosciutto (parma) ham or its Spanish cousin, serrano ham, in separate bowls. A bowl of rocket leaves would be great too.

Roast Red and Yellow Peppers

Serves 8–10

I adore having some good roast peppers in a kilner jar in the fridge to eat as part of a tapas plate like this or to throw on top of some freshly cooked pasta, in a salad, sandwich or whatever takes your fancy!

2 red peppers, left whole
2 yellow peppers, left whole
olive oil

Preheat the oven to 230°C/450°F/gas 8. Rub some olive oil over the peppers, then pop on a baking tray or glass plate and put into the hot oven. Cook for about 40 minutes or until very soft and a bit black. Take out of the oven, put into a bowl, cover with cling film and let cool. When cool, peel the skin off the peppers with your hands. Don't rinse in water, as you'll lose the flavour if you do. I find it helps to have a bowl of water nearby in which to rinse my hands. Using a butter knife, scrape the seeds out, which should leave just the flesh. Use as desired.

Marinated Olives

Make your own spiced or herbed olives by starting off with some really good black or green olives. I prefer to leave the stones in. Add some freshly ground spices. Fennel seeds, cumin seeds and coriander seeds all work well, either together or on their own. Add some chopped chilli or a pinch of dried chilli flakes and/or some chopped herbs, such as coriander, marjoram, oregano, rosemary, sage, parsley or thyme. Top up with a couple glugs of good-quality olive oil and store in a kilner/jam jar or even a tied plastic bag in the fridge, where they will easily keep for a month.

Basic Meringues

Makes 20–30 small meringues or 2 x 18 cm (7 in) discs

2 egg whites
125 g (4½ oz) icing sugar, sieved

Preheat the oven to 150°C/300°F/gas 2 and line a baking tray with greaseproof paper. Place the egg whites and the sieved icing sugar into a perfectly clean, dry bowl and using the highest speed possible on your electric beater or food mixer, whisk until the mixture forms stiff, dry peaks. If you're making the meringue specifically to break up into pieces for the Strawberry Meringue Pudding (page 37), then just spread the mixture out until it's about 1 cm (½ inch) thick all over. Alternatively, you could pipe out with a piping bag or drop spoonfuls onto the paper into tiny blobs. Place into the preheated oven and cook for 50–60 minutes or until the meringue easily lifts off the paper.

NOTE When the small meringues are cooked and cooled, try dipping the tops into melted chocolate and put back on the greaseproof paper, chocolate side up, to cool. You could also sandwich them with cream, raspberries and cream, strawberries and cream, cream flavoured with some grated orange zest or the Chocolate Cream Sauce on page 168-9.

Orange Spice Cakes

Makes 12 in a muffin tin or 20 in a standard bun tin

This recipe was inspired by Darina's Tunisian Orange Cake; she in turn was inspired by Sophie Grigson. If I was going to an outdoor picnic, I'd bring these along.

150 g (5½ oz) ground almonds, plus 10 g (½ oz) for dusting the tin
200 g (7 oz) caster sugar
200 ml (7 fl oz) sunflower or groundnut oil
4 eggs
finely grated zest of 1 orange
finely grated zest of ½ lemon

For the syrup:
juice of 1 orange
juice of ½ lemon
50 g (2 oz) sugar
2 cloves
6 cm (2 in) cinnamon stick

Preheat the oven to 180°C/350°F/gas 4. Grease the muffin tin and dust the inside with the 10 g (½ oz) of ground almonds. In a large bowl, mix the 150 g (5½ oz) of ground almonds and sugar. In a smaller, separate bowl, whisk the oil with the eggs and orange and lemon zest and add to the dry ingredients; stir to mix. Pour the rather wet mixture into the prepared tin and place in the oven. Cook for 20 minutes or until they are golden brown and set in the centre.

Meanwhile, make the syrup (it's not essential, but so good). Put all the ingredients into a small saucepan, stir as it comes up to the boil to dissolve the sugar and boil for 5 minutes, until it's a bit syrupy. When the cakes are cooked, wait for a few minutes before you take them out of the tin, then pierce each one a few times with a skewer. Place them on a serving plate, and while still hot pour the hot syrup over them.

NOTE Try serving these with crème fraîche or a dollop of greek yoghurt. Eat with a cup of coffee at the end of a meal, or bring along to a picnic.

NOTE These stay moist and juicy for a week, even two, stored in an airtight container.

NOTE I have also made these without the orange, in which case just double the lemon zest and juice. You can also leave out the spices if you like.

Strawberry Meringue Pudding

Serves 8

I suppose this is pretty much the same as Eton Mess. I haven't mashed the strawberries in this recipe, but you could.

250 ml (9 fl oz) cream
6 individual meringues (about 500 ml (18 fl oz) in volume), roughly broken up into 2–3 cm (¾–1 in) pieces (see recipe on page 35)
250 g (9 oz) strawberries, quartered
icing sugar, to serve

Whip the cream until thick, then add the broken-up meringues and quartered strawberries. Serve in little glasses and dust with icing sugar.

NOTE You could also use the Chocolate Meringues in this from page 168–9.

Crema Seville
(Orange Meringue Ice Cream)

Serves 8

My mother makes this excellent, quick ice cream. Its citrus zestiness is
a welcome treat after all the strong, intense flavours on the mezze
plate. This is also delicious unfrozen and just spooned into little glasses,
like the Strawberry Meringue Pudding on page 37.

250 ml (9 fl oz) cream
6 individual meringues (about 500 ml (18 fl oz) in volume),
roughly broken up into 2–3 cm (³/₄–1 in) pieces (see recipe on page 35)
1 orange, rind finely grated and juiced
30 ml (1 fl oz) Cointreau or Grand Marnier, though I don't think mum
uses a measure for this bit!

Whip the cream until thick, then mix in all the remaining ingredients.
Put into a bowl and freeze. Alternatively, if you want to turn this out,
put it into a loaf tin lined with a double layer of cling film, then turn it
out onto a plate and cut into slices to serve.

NOTE You basically need equal quantities of whipped cream and
meringue, but then your flavourings can vary (like the Strawberry
Meringue Pudding). If you're freezing it, though, some things work
better than others. Try the Toffee or Chocolate Sauce (page 109) swirled
through it, some Hazelnut Crunch (page 56) or just some plain toasted
chopped hazelnuts or almonds. A lot of fruit goes quite icey when
frozen, like strawberries, raspberries, etc.

NOTE You can drizzle a little Campari over the tops of these!

Mojito

Serves 2

This has to be one of my favourite cocktails.

2 tbsp light brown or granulated sugar
2 tbsp mint leaves
juice of 2 limes
8 ice cubes (optional)
100 ml (3½ fl oz) white rum, such as Bacardi
splash of soda water

Put two glasses in the freezer ahead of time. Put 1 tbsp of the sugar and 1 tbsp of the mint leaves in each frozen glass and crush with the back of a spoon, just enough to release the natural oils from the mint (you don't need the leaves to actually break up). Add the lime juice and ice, if using. Stir, then add the rum and a small splash of soda water, pop in a straw and drink!

NOTE If you're making a lot of this, you may want to crush the sugar and mint in a bowl with a pestle, or pop it into a plastic bag and bash it with a rolling pin.

Great Family Meals

I am always trying to think of food that both children and adults like, that doesn't take too much time to prepare and is nutritious at the same time. The food in this chapter is family friendly, yet would work for a dinner party too.

Pea and Coriander Soup

Serves 4–6

We make this soup at the cookery school. It's such a fast, great recipe and has to be one of my favourites.

50 g (2 oz) butter
150 g (5½ oz) onion, chopped
2 garlic cloves, chopped
1 red or green chilli, deseeded and chopped
salt and pepper
850 ml (1½ pints) chicken or vegetable stock
450 g (1 lb) peas (good frozen ones are fine)
2 tbsp chopped coriander

Melt the butter in a large saucepan, then add the onion, garlic and chilli and season with salt and pepper. Cover with a butter wrapper or greaseproof paper, put on the lid and sweat over a low heat for 3 or 4 minutes or until the onions are cooked. Then add the stock, turn up the heat to high and bring up to the boil. Add the peas and cook very rapidly, making sure to remove the lid as soon as it comes to the boil (this keeps the peas' fresh green colour intact) for only 1 or 2 minutes or until the peas are cooked. Add the coriander and immediately liquidise. Check seasoning and serve.

NOTE Like most soups, this freezes really well.

NOTE Avoid prolonged boiling and simmering of this soup to retain the fresh green colour.

Stock

Makes about 2 litre (3½ pt)

Making stock is actually incredibly easy. It takes only 5 minutes to throw everything into the pot, then just let it cook for a while and you're already halfway there to a good, nutritious soup.

bones from 1 chicken (leave out for vegetable stock)
1–2 carrots
1 onion or 1 leek
1 stick of celery
1 small bay leaf
sprig of parsley or thyme

If you're making chicken stock, break up your chicken bones, if you can. They could be raw (but with the blood removed/washed off) or cooked (such as the carcass from a whole roast chicken). For a vegetable stock, just omit the chicken. Put the chicken into a large pot and add the carrots, onion or leek, celery, bay leaf and parsley or thyme. You could even just use the ends of the carrots, onion peelings, celery leaves, any leftover mushrooms, the green bits of the leek that you've discarded, trimmings from a fennel bulb...you get the picture. Don't bother with potato, they just make the stock cloudy and don't give it much flavour.

Fill up the pot with cold water and bring up to the boil. Simmer for 1 or 2 hours, or you can put it into the oven at 140°C/275°F/gas 1. Strain the stock when you're happy with the flavour and discard all the bits. Skim the fat off the stock as it cools. Stock will only keep in the fridge for 2 or 3 days at best, but it freezes perfectly. Clean out plastic milk containers and freeze the stock in those. (I would then write chicken or vegetable stock on them with indelible pen.) Then if you're in a hurry you can cut these plastic containers open and quickly defrost the stock in a saucepan. If you have a small freezer, then keep the stock on the heat with the lid off for an extra hour or so and it will reduce down to a strongly flavoured stock, but be careful not to let it burn. When it's good and strong – much stronger than you would normally want it to be – strain it (if you haven't already) and degrease it as it cools, then pour it into an ice cube tray or bag and freeze. Then you'll have your very own homemade stock cubes in the freezer!

Smoked Mackerel Pâté

Serves 6

It's great to have some of this in the fridge for snacks on the run or a packed lunch. It's lovely and light and will keep for a week. Of course, the better the smoked mackerel, the better the pâté. For a family meal I put a kilner jar of this on a big board with lots of crusty bread or toast in the middle of the table and let everyone dig in while the rest of the meal (if you're having anything else, because frankly it's almost enough on its own) is being prepared.

100 g (3½ oz) smoked mackerel, about 1 fillet
75 g (2¾ oz) cream cheese
75 g (2¾ oz) crème fraîche
juice of ½ lemon
salt and pepper

In a food processor, whiz up the smoked mackerel, then add the cream cheese and the crème fraîche. Empty into a bowl and fold in the lemon juice, salt and pepper to taste.

Quick Roast Chicken with Lemon and Spices

Serves 4–6, depending on the size of chicken and what you decide to serve with it

You can make this and pop it into the oven straight away or you can have it marinating in the fridge all day. Then all you have to do in the evening is throw it into the hot oven, and 25 minutes later it's ready. Easy!

1 chicken, jointed into 8 pieces
grated rind and juice of 1 lemon
1 head of garlic, peeled but cloves left whole
seeds of 10 green cardamom pods, crushed
1 tsp ground coriander seeds
¼–½ tsp chilli flakes
½ tsp ground turmeric
50 ml (2 fl oz) olive oil

Put the chicken pieces into a bowl. In a separate bowl, mix the rest of the ingredients together, then add to the chicken. Toss with your hands to cover the chicken with the spicy marinade. Leave to marinate for 1–2 hours, if possible.

There are two ways to cook the chicken here. You could cook it directly in the spicy marinade for 1 hour at 150°C/300°F/ gas 2. This results in a lovely, juicy dish giving everyone enough spicy 'gravy' to pour over the chicken when eating. Or you could cook the chicken quite quickly without the marinade in the oven preheated to 240°C/475°F/gas 9 for 25 minutes. This will give you a crispy result without much juice, but delicious all the same. Either way, sprinkle salt over the chicken just before it goes in the oven. If you put the salt in the marinade from the beginning the chicken tends to dry out a bit. Serve with Basmati Rice (page 80), Lemon Roast Potatoes (page 64) or Orzo (page 167) and Cucumber Raita (below).

NOTE This recipe is excellent cooked on the barbeque.

Cucumber Raita

Makes 450 ml (16 fl oz)

250 g (9 oz) tub of greek yoghurt
½ cucumber, deseeded and finely diced
2 tbsp chopped coriander or mint
salt and pepper
4 tomatoes (optional)

Put the yoghurt into a bowl, add the cucumber, coriander and some salt and pepper to taste. Chopped tomatoes can also be added into this.

NOTE You could also grate the whole cucumber for this, but first sprinkle it with a pinch of salt and let it drain sitting in a sieve over a bowl for 10 minutes to get rid of excess juices.

Great Family Meals

Quick Roast Chicken with Red Onions, Garlic, Carrots, Leeks and New Potatoes

Serves 4–6 people, depending on the chicken

This recipe came about by necessity when I was trying to figure out how to get the chicken cooked as quickly as possible for my screaming, hungry children, and thankfully it was a success!

1 chicken, jointed into 8 pieces
1 large or 2 small red onions, cut into 6 or 8 wedges from the top to the root
4–10 cloves of garlic, depending on your taste, peeled
2–4 carrots, peeled (or just scrubbed) and cut into 2 cm (¾ in) chunks
(leave whole if they're baby carrots)
1 leek, cut into chunks
12 small new potatoes, scrubbed
80 ml (3 fl oz) olive oil
sea salt and pepper

Preheat the oven to 240°C/475°F/gas 9. Put the chicken pieces, red onions, garlic, carrots, leeks and potatoes into a large bowl. Pour over the olive oil, season with some sea salt and pepper and toss together with your hands. Add more olive oil if it's a bit dry. Spread out in a single layer on a baking/roasting tray and pop into the hot oven for 25 minutes or until the chicken is cooked and the skin is crispy.

NOTE Feel free to vary the vegetables in this or just leave them out altogether and serve them separately. If you want to use old potatoes, just scrub them well and cut into quarters.

NOTE Herbs like sage, rosemary or thyme are good in this. Just add in whole sprigs 5 minutes before the end of cooking.

Roast Potato Wedges

Serves 4-6

Fast roast potatoes, in and out of the oven in about 25 minutes.

*1 kg (2¼ lb) potatoes, scrubbed well. I don't normally peel for this,
though you can
50 ml (2 fl oz) olive oil
sea salt and freshly ground pepper*

Preheat the oven to 230°C/450°F/gas 8. Cut the potatoes into wedges
and thoroughly dry them all over with kitchen paper. Put them in a
bowl and drizzle with enough olive oil to coat them evenly, toss with
your hands and season with sea salt and pepper. Place in a single layer
on a baking tray and pop into the hot oven. Cook until the potatoes
are soft on the inside and crisp on the outside, about 25 minutes.

NOTE If these need to keep warm for any amount of time in the oven,
don't cover them.

NOTE For spicy potato wedges, sprinkle with ½ –1 tsp chilli powder or
dried chilli flakes.

NOTE You can also add whole garlic cloves (peeled or not) halfway
through cooking, and whole rosemary or thyme sprigs are good too,
also added in halfway through cooking.

Shepherd's Pie

Serves 5–6

I think this has to be one of the best family foods, but don't underestimate it as a great dinner party main course. You can even replace the lamb with minced beef (for a cottage pie) or with cooked, chopped duck meat.

50 g (1¾ oz) butter
2 onions, chopped
salt and pepper
1 kg (2 lb 4 oz) minced lamb, not too lean, or minced cooked lamb left over from a roast
250 ml (9 fl oz) lamb or chicken stock
2 tbsp roux (see recipe on page 66)
1–2 tbsp Ballymaloe Country Relish or something similar
mashed potatoes made with 1 kg (2 lb 4 oz) potatoes, as on page 52, but without the mustard
garlic butter, to serve

Preheat the grill in the oven. Melt the butter in a large saucepan. Add the chopped onions, season with salt and pepper, cover with a butter wrapper or a disc of greaseproof paper and a lid and cook on a gentle heat until soft but not coloured. Add the mince, increase the heat and cook, stirring regularly, for a few minutes until the meat changes colour. Pour in the stock, bring to the boil, decrease the heat and cover with a lid and continue to cook for about 20 minutes or until the meat is cooked, taking care not to let it burn on the bottom (you can also put it into the oven at 160°C/325°F/gas 3).

Strain the liquid off the meat, pour back into the saucepan and bring back up to the boil. Add 1 tbsp of the roux and whisk until the juices have thickened. Whisk in more roux if it isn't thick enough. Pour the

Great Family Meals

juices back in with the meat and add the relish and some salt and pepper to taste.

Pour into a large pie dish or individual dishes. Place the mashed potato on top, score with a fork and put it under a hot grill to brown the potato slightly. If preparing the pie in advance, when ready to eat put the shepherd's pie into a moderate oven (180°C/350°F/gas 4) for 15–25 minutes, until hot and bubbling. Serve with a few pats of garlic butter melting on top.

NOTE If you would like the potato to be very golden on top, add 1 beaten egg or 1 egg yolk to the mashed potato with the butter when mashing it.

Garlic Butter

Makes 100 g (3½ oz)

A pat of this butter is excellent on top of a cooked steak.

100 g (3½ oz) softened butter
3–4 cloves of garlic, crushed
2 tbsp chopped parsley
1 tsp lemon juice

Mix all the ingredients together and roll up in some parchment paper or cling film, or just put into a bowl. If you wrap it in paper, stick it in the freezer and cut off slices as needed. Just be sure to write what's in the butter if you decide to make different logs with different flavours (see below).

NOTE The possibilities for flavoured butters are endless. You could add marjoram to the garlic butter, coriander and chilli butter for a chicken breast, finely chopped olives and anchovies on a lamb chop, sun-dried tomatoes and basil butter on chicken or in a bit of pasta at the end, stirred through to melt.

Lamb Chops with Mustard Mash and Garlic and Parsley Peas

Serves 4-6

I love the combination of the hot mustard mash with slightly sweet lamb chops and garlicky peas.

lamb chops (2–3 per person)
olive oil
sea salt and freshly ground black pepper

Remove excess fat from the chops, but leave ½ cm still on. Drizzle with olive oil and freshly ground black pepper. Place a frying pan or grill pan on a high heat. When it's good and hot add the lamb chops and sprinkle with a little sea salt and more freshly ground pepper. Cook for approximately 3 minutes on each side. Remove to a plate, cover and rest in a warm oven for 5 minutes.

Garlic and Parsley Peas

Serves 4–6

50 g (1¾ oz) butter
2 tbsp chopped parsley
2–4 cloves of garlic, crushed
a small squeeze of lemon juice
450 g (1 lb) peas, straight from the freezer if you like

Melt the butter in a hot frying or sauté pan. Add the parsley, garlic, lemon juice and the peas and cook on a high heat for about 2 minutes, until the peas are cooked.

Mustard Mash

Serves 4–6

1 kg (2¼ lb) potatoes (new potatoes are too waxy for this)
50 g (1¾ oz) butter
200 ml (7 fl oz) milk, or 150 ml (5 fl oz) milk and 50 ml (2 fl oz) cream,
boiling
2–3 tbsp Dijon mustard
salt and pepper

I find this is the best way to cook good, fluffy, floury potatoes. Clean
the potatoes and put them into a saucepan of cold water with a good
pinch of salt. Bring the water up to the boil and cook for 10 minutes.
Pour all but 4 cm (1½ in) of the water out and continue to cook the
potatoes on a very low heat. Don't be tempted to stick a knife into
them, the skins will break and they'll just break up and get soggy if you
do. About 20 minutes later, when you think the potatoes might be
cooked, test them with a skewer: if they're soft, take them off the heat.

Peel the potatoes while they're still hot and mash them immediately.
To peel them while hot, hold them in a tea towel (not your fancy ones).
Add the butter, but don't add any milk until they're free of lumps.
When the potatoes are mashed, add the boiling milk (or milk and
cream). You might not need it all or you might need more, it depends
on the potatoes. Add the Dijon mustard to taste and some salt and
pepper. If you want to make this in advance, add a little extra milk, as
the potatoes dry out as they sit. It will keep well in a warm oven – just
keep it covered with a lid, plate or tin foil.

Brown Scones with Seeds

Makes 12 scones

225 g (8 oz) wholemeal flour
225 g (8 oz) plain white flour
25 g (1 oz) sesame seeds
25 g (1 oz) pumpkin seeds
25 g (1 oz) golden linseeds or hemp seeds
25 g (1 oz) sunflower seeds
1 tsp salt
1 tsp bread soda, finely sieved
25 g (1 oz) butter
1 egg, whisked
400 ml (14 fl oz) buttermilk

Preheat the oven to 220°C/425°F/gas 7. In a big bowl mix together the brown and white flour, the seeds, salt and the sieved bread soda. Rub in the butter with your fingers. In a separate bowl, whisk the egg with the buttermilk and pour most of the liquid into the dry ingredients. Using one hand with your fingers open and stiff, mix in a full circle, bringing the flour and liquid together, adding more liquid if necessary. The dough should be quite soft, but not too sticky.

Turn the dough out onto a floured surface. Don't knead it, but rather gently bring it into a ball. Flatten it slightly to about 4 cm (1½ in) high. Cut the dough into square scones. If you like you could brush any leftover liquid over the tops and sprinkle with some extra seeds.

Put the scones onto a baking tray, pop into the hot oven and cook for 15–25 minutes (depending on the size of the scones). Have a look at them after 10 minutes; if they're already deep golden brown, then turn the heat down to 200°C/400°F/gas 6 for the remainder of the time. When cooked they should sound hollow when tapped. Cool on a wire rack.

Apple Fudge Cake

Serves 10

My sister-in-law, Penny, makes this cake. It's perfect as a dessert or with a cup of tea or coffee. Sooooo good.

2 large cooking apples, such as Brambleys
50 g (1¾ oz) dark brown sugar

cake batter:
175 g (6 oz) butter
175 g (6 oz) light brown sugar
175 g (6 oz) self-raising flour
4 eggs

fudge sauce:
110 g (4 oz) butter
110 g (4 oz) light brown sugar
1 tbsp lemon juice

You will also need a 25 cm (10 in) sauté pan or a springform tin.

Preheat the oven to 180°C/350°F/gas 4. Butter the sides of the tin and line the base with a disc of greaseproof paper. Peel and cut the apples into eights and arrange in a single layer in the tin (this will be the top of the cake when it's cooked). Sprinkle over the 50 g (2 oz) dark brown sugar.

Put all the cake batter ingredients into a food processor and whiz to combine. Pour it over the apples and sugar. Cook in the preheated oven for 40–45 minutes or until the cake is spongey in the centre. Wait for it to cool for 2 minutes before turning out.

Next make the fudge sauce. Combine and melt the butter, sugar and lemon juice. Stir and pour over the cake when it's cool.

Tuscan (Upside-Down) Plum Tart

Serves 10

I am indebted to Darina for this recipe.

275 g (9½ oz) sugar
150 ml (5 fl oz) water
900 g (2 lb) plums (or peaches or nectarines – they work equally well)
150 g (5½ oz) soft butter
175 g (6 oz) sugar
200 g (7 oz) self-raising flour
3 eggs

You will also need a 25 cm (10 in) sauté pan or frying pan that can be used in the oven.

Preheat the oven to 170°C/325°F/gas 3. Put the sugar and water into the pan. Stir over a medium heat until the sugar dissolves, then cook without stirring until the sugar caramelises to a golden brown. Meanwhile, halve and stone the plums. When the sugar is done, pour it into the pan, then carefully arrange the plums cut side down in a single layer over the caramel (this will be the top of the cake when it's cooked).

Put the butter, sugar and flour into the bowl of an electric food processor, whiz for a couple of seconds, then add the eggs and stop as soon as the mixture comes together. (If you don't have a food processor, just cream the butter and sugar, add the eggs one by one, then mix in the flour.) Spread the mixture in an even layer over the plums in the pan. Bake in the preheated oven for about 1 hour. The centre should be firm to the touch and the edges should be slightly shrunk from the sides of the pan. Run a knife around the edges to make sure it hasn't stuck anywhere. Leave it to sit for 3 or 4 minutes before turning out. Serve with whipped cream or crème fraîche.

Banana and Hazelnut Crunch Ice Cream

Serves 8

You can leave the hazelnut crunch out if you prefer, or just use it to sprinkle over the top. This has to be the quickest ice cream. I love it!

hazelnut crunch:
150 g (5½ oz) sugar
150 g (5½ oz) toasted, peeled hazelnuts (I buy them like this from the health food shop)

banana ice cream:
4 bananas (650 g (1½ lb) with skins, 400 g (14 oz) without skins)
juice of ½ lemon
175 g (6 oz) sugar
500 ml (18 fl oz) cream

To make the hazelnut crunch, put the sugar and hazelnuts into a non-stick frying pan or a medium saucepan and place over a medium heat. Cook until the sugar has caramelised to a deep golden brown. Don't stir the mixture at any time, but you can tilt and slightly shake the pan a bit if it's cooking unevenly. Pour it out onto a non-stick baking tray or a tray lined with a sheet of parchment paper. Leave to cool and harden. When it has hardened, whiz it up in a food processor so it's still nice and crunchy, or just put it into a plastic bag and bash it with a rolling pin. This keeps for a month or so in a kilner jar and is great sprinkled over any ice cream.

For the ice cream, liquidise the bananas, lemon juice and sugar (or whiz in a food processor). Add the cream and pulse to mix. Place in a bowl and put into the freezer. When it's semi-frozen, after about 2 hours, fold in all but a few tablespoons of the hazelnut crunch (keep the rest for sprinkling over the top when serving the ice cream). Place back in the freezer and continue to freeze.

  Great Family Meals

If you want to leave out the hazelnut crunch, still take the ice cream out of the freezer when it's semi-frozen and whisk it for a couple of seconds, put it back into the freezer and continue to freeze.

When serving this ice cream, take it out of the freezer 30 minutes before serving and put it in the fridge. It will be much easier to scoop.

Raspberry Lemonade

Serves 8

This is so fresh and zesty, though do try it sometime with white wine or sparkling wine. If you want to make this ahead of time don't add the water/wine until you're ready to serve it.

250 g (9 oz) raspberries
100–125 g (3½ –4½ oz) sugar
finely grated rind and juice of 2 lemons
500 ml (18 fl oz) water, sparkling or still (white wine or sparkling wine is also fab!)

In a food processor or blender, whiz the raspberries and sugar, then strain through a sieve into a pitcher to remove the seeds. Add the lemon juice, rind and the water. Add some ice and serve.

When the Boat Comes In

There are so many exciting ways of cooking good, fresh fish,
from little Spicy Crab Cakes served with Thai Dipping Sauce to
a delicious creamy Fish Pie with clouds of mashed potato to the
unbeatable simple Pan-Fried Fish drizzled with a squeeze of
lemon juice, which for me has to be the ultimate fast food.

Spicy Crab Cakes with Thai Dipping Sauce

Makes 50 mini crab cakes for little bites to serve with drinks or 12 bigger ones

If it's possible for you to get brown crab meat as well as the white meat, do, but these are still good with just white meat.

110 g (4 oz) butter
4 tbsp white wine
4 cloves of garlic, crushed or finely grated
450 g (1 lb) crab meat
200 g (7 oz) white breadcrumbs
1 egg, whisked
1 tbsp Dijon mustard
3 tbsp chopped coriander (you can chop the small stalks too)
6 spring onions, chopped
1 tbsp Worcestershire sauce
½ tbsp Tabasco sauce (or 1 deseeded and chopped chilli)
½ tbsp soy sauce

Melt the butter in a pan with the wine and garlic, add the crab meat and cook for 3 minutes, stirring occasionally. Season with salt and pepper. Combine all the other ingredients in a bowl, then add the crab meat and all the juices from the pan and mix to combine. Shape into 12 patties or little balls for mini ones and either deep fry or pan fry in some olive oil until nice and golden (I normally cook them in a pan). Serve with Thai Dipping Sauce (page 60). These are also good with Tomato Salsa (page 78) or Sweet Chilli Mayonnaise (page 105).

Thai Dipping Sauce

Makes 250 ml (9 fl oz)

This is a fantastic dipping sauce to use with grilled or deep-fried fish, meat or spring rolls.

100 ml (3½ fl oz) nam pla (Thai fish sauce, widely available now)
100 ml (3½ fl oz) freshly squeezed lime or lemon juice (about 2 limes or
1 lemon, but measure to be sure)
75 g (2¾ oz) caster sugar
2 cloves garlic, crushed or finely grated
3–6 hot red or green chillies, sliced into fine rounds

Take out the chilli seeds if you like, though for this I would leave them in. To deseed a whole chilli, cut off the stalk at the top. With the cut side facing down onto your work surface, hold the chilli vertically between your hands and roll the chilli between your hands. The seeds should fall out the cut end.

To make the sauce, combine the fish sauce, lime or lemon juice, sugar, garlic and sliced chillies in a jar or bowl and stir to dissolve the sugar.

NOTE If you find this too strong, add 50 ml (2 fl oz) of water.

Pan-Fried Fish with Chilli and Parsley Oil or Salsa Verde

Serves 2 as a main course or 4 as a starter

The trick to really good pan-fried fish is fresh fish. Fresh fish should not and does not have a strong smell – it should be lightly fragrant of the sea.

4 fillets of flat fish, such as John Dory, plaice, sole, brill or turbot,
or part of a round fish fillet, like salmon, cod, grey mullet, etc.
(allow 175 g (6 oz) for a main course and 75 g (2¾ oz) for a starter)
olive oil
seasoned flour, i.e. with a pinch of salt and pepper (optional)
25 g (1 oz) butter, softened (optional)

Dry the fish fillets on kitchen paper. Heat a cast iron or non-stick frying pan on a high heat (stainless steel sticks) until smoking. Add a dash of olive oil and throw in the fish fillets. Turn when golden on one side, then cook again until golden on the other side. Drizzle with Chilli and Parsley Oil or Salsa Verde (see page 68) or a squeeze of lemon juice and serve immediately.

NOTE If you want to use the seasoned flour and butter (as above), then dip the fillets in the seasoned flour and spread a little soft butter on one side of the fish. Put that side down in the hot pan first, and cook as above.

NOTE You can skin the fillets if you like.

Mussels Steamed in Coconut Milk with Lime and Coriander

Serves 10 as a starter or 6 as a main course

I absolutely love a big bowl of these steaming mussels. They're good for a starter or a main course served with some Roast Garlic Bread.

1 large onion, chopped
5–10 cloves of garlic (I use 10!), crushed
2 red or green chillies, deseeded and chopped
400 g (14 oz) tin of coconut milk
1–2 tbsp nam pla (Thai fish sauce)
juice of 1 lime
1 tbsp chopped coriander
80 mussels, scrubbed

Put everything but the mussels into a saucepan large enough to hold the mussels. Bring up to the boil and cook for about 8 minutes or until the onions are cooked. Meanwhile, check that all the mussels are tightly closed. If one is open, tap it and if it closes it's good, so keep it, but if any stay open then throw those ones out since that means they're dead and you don't know how fresh they are.

When the onions are cooked in the saucepan, throw in all the good mussels, put the lid on and cook until the mussels are wide open. Serve the mussels in their shells with the coconut broth. Divine! This is great with the Roast Garlic Bread. For a main course you could serve rice as an accompaniment. Don't forget to have finger bowls and a spare bowl for discarded shells.

NOTE Without the mussels, this sauce keeps well in the fridge for a couple of days, so if you want you could take out the sauce as you

need it (1 ladleful per person). Then put it into a saucepan and add
however many mussels you like (about 8 for a starter and 12–15 for
a main course), put on the heat and cook as above.

Roast Garlic Bread

Serves 6

175 g (6 oz) butter
6–8 cloves of garlic, crushed or grated
2 tbsp chopped parsley
1 baguette

Preheat the oven to 230°C/450°F/gas 7. In a saucepan, melt the butter,
then add the garlic and chopped parsley. Cut the baguette horizontally
and generously brush the melted garlic butter over the cut sides. Put
on a baking tray and place in the hot oven for 8–10 minutes or until
toasted and golden brown. This freezes perfectly, but don't roast it first.

Lemon Roast Potatoes

Serves 4–6

If serving the green beans (page 69), I wouldn't serve these too. I would serve plain roast potato wedges so as not to have citrus overkill!

6 large potatoes, peeled
2 lemons
olive oil
salt and pepper

Preheat the oven to 220°C/425°F/gas 7. Chop the potatoes into 2–3 cm (¾–1 in) cubes and dry well with kitchen paper. Slice the lemons quite thickly, then cut those slices into 1–2 cm (½–¾ in) chunks. Put into a bowl with the potatoes and, using your hands, slightly squeeze the lemon with the potatoes to release a bit of juice. Drizzle with a couple tablespoons of olive oil, add salt and pepper and put in a single layer on a baking/roasting tray in the oven until cooked, about 20 minutes. Empty the contents of the tray out onto a serving dish. You can eat the lemon bits if you like, but they've also given the potatoes a fresh citrus flavour.

Falafel in Warm Pitta Bread

Lamb Chop with Mustard Mash and Garlic and Parsley Peas

Mussels Steamed in Coconut Milk with Lime and Coriander

Pan-Fried Fish with Chilli and Parsley Oil

Making Rodeo Wraps

Shepherd's Pie

Apple Fudge Cake

Dill Pesto

Makes 125 ml (4 fl oz)

4 tbsp chopped dill
2 cloves of garlic, crushed
50 ml (2 fl oz) olive oil
salt to taste

For the pesto, whiz all the ingredients together in a food processor and season to taste. Add more olive oil if it seems too thick.

Roast Cherry Tomatoes

Serves 4

500g (1 lb 2 oz) or 20 cherry tomatoes (they look nice if they're still on the vine)
sea salt and pepper
a pinch of sugar
olive oil

Preheat the oven to 230°C/450°F/gas 8. Drizzle the tomatoes with a little olive oil and season (still on the vine, you can cut the stalks in half with some scissors to portion them) with salt, pepper and sugar. Put into a hot oven and roast for 8–10 minutes or until they are soft and just about to burst.

Fish Pie

Serves 6–8

Obviously, the fresher the fish, the better the fish pie. You can also use decent frozen fish.

1 kg (2¼ lbs) skinned fish fillets, such as hake, cod, whiting,
grey sea mullet, ling, etc.
200 ml (7 fl oz) white wine (use the wine you may be opening to drink
with this; it'll be worth it if it's drinkable – don't use a bad cooking wine)
200 ml (7 fl oz) water
200 ml (7 fl oz) cream
200 g (7 oz) cheddar cheese, grated (optional)
200 g (7 oz) peas, cooked in a tiny bit of boiling water for 2 minutes
200 g (7 oz) mushrooms, sliced and sautéed in a little butter

roux:
50 g (2 oz) butter
50 g (1¾ oz) flour

buttered crumbs (optional):
25 g (1 oz) butter
50 g (1¾ oz) white breadcrumbs

Cut the fish into portions. If you have a thin little piece of fish, fold it over, in two. Place the portions of fish in a single layer in a wide pan, season with salt and pepper and cover with the wine and water. Put the lid on and cook on a medium heat for about 8 minutes or until the fish is just cooked. Carefully remove the fish from the pan and set aside.

Add the cream to the liquid in the pan and place on a high heat with no lid. Boil until it has reduced down a bit and you're happy with the flavour.

When the Boat Comes In

To make the roux, in a separate pan melt the butter, add the flour and cook for 2 minutes. Add 1 or 2 tsp of the roux to start with to the cream sauce while it is simmering and whisk. Add more roux only if it needs it; it shouldn't be too thick. Take the cream sauce off the heat and whisk in three-quarters of the cheese, if using. Add the peas and mushrooms and taste for seasoning.

Pour some sauce into your serving dish. Add the fish, being careful not to break it up, and cover with the remaining sauce. If you want a crunchy top, melt 25 g (1 oz) butter and mix with 50 g (1¾ oz) white breadcrumbs. Then mix the remaining one-quarter of the grated cheese with the buttered crumbs and scatter over the top. Reheat in a moderate oven (180°C/350°F/gas 4) until it's hot and bubbling, about 10–20 minutes. Serve a salad after this if you like.

You have a few choices here. You could serve it like the Shepherd's Pie (page 48) with a layer of mashed potato on top, or you could serve mashed potatoes or new potatoes on the side. You could also serve a bowl of rice, or if you have a piping bag you could pipe mashed potato all around the sides of the bowl.

NOTE Roux keeps in the fridge for weeks.

NOTE If you want to reheat this, or indeed even freeze it, make sure the fish is only just cooked, because it will cook a bit more in the reheating.

NOTE If you want to serve this immediately and omit the buttered crumbs, just keep the fish warm while you finish the sauce, then pour the sauce over the fish and serve.

Chilli and Parsley Oil

Makes 150 ml (5 fl oz)

1 handful of parsley leaves, roughly chopped
2 cloves of garlic, crushed
1 red chilli, deseeded and chopped
sea salt and freshly ground black pepper
90 ml (3 fl oz) olive oil

Put the parsley, garlic and chilli into a bowl, season with salt and pepper and add enough olive oil to make a loose sauce.

NOTE Great with pan-fried scallops, squid, prawns, lamb chops and steak. Also good served as a quick pasta sauce.

NOTE This easily keeps for a couple of weeks in the fridge.

Salsa Verde

Makes 150 ml (5 fl oz)

1 handful of parsley leaves
grated zest and juice of 1 small lemon
2 cloves of garlic, crushed
1 tbsp capers, rinsed
50 ml (2 fl oz) olive oil
black pepper

Put the parsley, lemon zest, garlic and capers into a food processor and whiz until it's all finely chopped. Add the lemon juice and olive oil (add more oil if you want it a bit more runny). Check the seasoning – it might not need salt, as the capers can be quite salty.

NOTE Salsa verde also keeps in the fridge for weeks.

NOTE This is fab with pasta, but is also excellent with a steak, a lamb chop or even a pan-fried chicken breast.

Green Beans with Lemon Juice, Sea Salt and Olive Oil

Serves 4–6

Not only is this good hot, served with fish or chicken, but it's also great served at room temperature. You can also use it as a base for a fresh light salad – add thinly sliced red onions, some cannellini beans or chickpeas (drained from the tin), tinned tuna and crumbled feta cheese for a fabulous and nutritious packed lunch (also good in a pitta bread).

500 ml (18 fl oz) water
1 level tsp salt
500 g (1 lb 2 oz) French beans
50 ml (2 fl oz) olive oil
juice of ¼–½ a lemon
sea salt and freshly ground pepper

Put the water and salt into a saucepan and bring to a boil. Top and tail the beans and cut in half at an angle. Add to the boiling water and put the lid back on until the water comes back to the boil. As soon as it does, take the lid off to keep the beans' bright green colour and continue to cook on a high heat until the beans are just cooked, but still have a bit of a bite. Drain and immediately add the olive oil, lemon juice and sea salt and pepper to taste. You must dress the beans while hot so that they soak up the fresh citrus flavour.

Prawn and Saffron Risotto with Dill Pesto

Serves 6

Isaac and I ate something a little bit like this in a restaurant called
Kampa Park in Prague. When we got home, Isaac created this: it's fab
and seriously rich!

1–1.2 litre (1¾–2 pt) light chicken stock
150 g (5½ oz) butter
4 cloves of garlic, crushed or finely grated
90 ml (3 fl oz) white wine
20–25 prawns, shelled
1 onion, finely chopped
400 g (14 oz) risotto rice (Arborio, Roma Carnaroli or Maratelli)
50 g (1¾ oz) freshly grated parmesan cheese
salt and pepper
10 strands of saffron

Put the chicken stock into a saucepan and bring to a simmer. Keep it
gently simmering away while you make the risotto. Make sure that the
stock isn't at a rolling boil for the 35 minutes or so that it will take to
cook the rice, otherwise it will reduce a lot and be very strong.

Melt half the butter in a frying pan with the garlic and 2 tbsp of the
white wine. Add the prawns and cook in the garlic butter for 4–5 minutes.
Remove the prawns to a plate and set aside. Cook the onion in the
remaining butter on a low heat with the lid on, then remove the lid
and add the rice and saffron and cook for a minute, stirring, then add
the last of the white wine and boil for a few minutes until most of the
wine has evaporated. Add a ladleful of simmering stock (about 150
ml/5 fl oz) to the rice and season with some salt and pepper. Cook
gently until this liquid has been absorbed, then add another ladleful
of stock. Repeat this process until the rice is just cooked and the texture

is how you want it. I like my risotto not too wet and not too stiff, a bit like porridge. You might not need all the stock or you might need a little extra. Add the parmesan and the prawns in garlic butter and serve in bowls with a drizzle of Dill Pesto (page 65) over the top.

NOTE If you really need to, you can make a risotto ahead of time. Just cook the rice three-quarters of the way and continue to finish cooking the rice when you intend to serve it. It will be much better if you wait until you are just about to serve it to add the prawns.

Fennel Gratin

Serves 4–6

3 large (or 5 small) fennel bulbs (about 800 g/1 lb 11 oz)
25 g (1 oz) butter
50 g (1¾ oz) white breadcrumbs
25 g (1 oz) grated parmesan cheese

Preheat the oven to 200°C/400°F/gas 6. Cut the stalky top off the fennel and trim the base. Cut the fennel bulbs in half lengthwise, and cook in boiling salted water for 10–15 minutes until just cooked. Remove from the water and let cool for a minute. Slice the fennel lengthwise again, about ½ cm (¼ in) thick. Place the overlapping slices on top of each other in a gratin dish. Melt the butter, mix in the breadcrumbs and then the grated parmesan. Sprinkle the cheesy buttered crumbs over the fennel and put it into the oven for 10–15 minutes, or until it is bubbling hot and the top is nicely golden and crunchy.

NOTE You can prepare this ahead of time up to the point of putting it into the oven.

NOTE Make the breadcrumbs by whizzing up white bread (a bit stale is perfect) in a food processor or even a liquidiser. You can remove the crusts first, if you like. Freezes perfectly.

NOTE If you would like a creamy fennel gratin, pour 75 ml (3 fl oz) cream over the fennel in the gratin dish before you add the crumbs.

When the Boat Comes In

Panna Cotta with Raspberries

Serves 4-6

Panna cotta has a silky, velvety texture. It's absolutely wonderful served with fresh raspberries or strawberries.

300 ml (10 fl oz) cream
25 g (1 oz) caster sugar
1 vanilla pod, with a small split, just enough to let out some seeds and a subtle flavour
1 leaf of gelatine

Put the cream, sugar and vanilla pod in a saucepan and slowly bring up to a simmer. Turn off the heat and leave to infuse.

Meanwhile, put the gelatine leaf into a bowl with just enough water to cover it. After 3–4 minutes it will have softened completely. At that point, take it out of the water and put into the saucepan with the hot cream. Whisk gently until the gelatine dissolves. If the cream has cooled down too much you might need to reheat it slightly with the gelatine. Pour into ramekins, pretty glasses, little cups or whatever you fancy. Leave for 2 hours in the fridge to set. Serve with raspberries or some gorgeous, sweet strawberries.

NOTE Panna cotta should be quite soft and wobbly in consistency, but if you like you can turn it out. Just oil the ramekin with a little sunflower oil before you pour in the mixture if you want to turn it out.

NOTE Panna cotta is normally made with 100 per cent cream, but if you want a slightly lighter panna cotta, use half milk, half cream or ¾ cream and ¼ milk.

NOTE You can use powdered gelatine instead of leaf, just follow the instructions on the box. 1 leaf = 1 rounded tsp.

Little Lemon Creams

Serves 10

These are simple, sweet little lemon puddings. You could serve them with Jane's Biscuits or macaroons (page 152 and 24) if you like, though they aren't essential.

500 ml (18 fl oz) cream
140 g (5 oz) caster sugar
juice of 2 lemons

Put the cream and sugar in a saucepan, bring to the boil and boil for 3 minutes. Remove from the heat, whisk in the lemon juice and pour into little cups, glasses or bowls and chill for 3 hours to set.

NOTE If you want to make these more zesty, just grate the rind of 1 lemon and mix with the lemon juice to add into the boiled cream and sugar.

NOTE To make little orange creams, replace the juice of 2 lemons with the grated rind and juice of 1 orange.

Peach and Mango Frappé

Serves 2-3

This is actually a very healthy cocktail to drink – at least that's what I always tell myself!

50 g (1¾ oz) caster sugar
50 ml (2 fl oz) boiling water
300 ml (10 fl oz) ice
110 g (4 oz) chopped mango flesh (½ medium mango)
110 g (4 oz) chopped peach (1 large peach)
100 ml (3½ fl oz) white rum, such as Bacardi (or more if you like!)
1½ tbsp lime juice

Dissolve the sugar in the boiling water to make a syrup. Let cool. Place in a blender with the remaining ingredients and blend until smooth. Serve in frozen tall glasses.

Chilli Night

Chillies are quite addictive, raising the natural endorphins in your body to make you feel good and happy, and they're good for you too! The key is not to use too many for your taste buds. Start off by using just a little and increase if you like. The seeds are the hottest part of the chilli, so you can leave them in if you like a serious kick. If you do get chilli burn, 1 tsp of sugar is a good antidote, and don't forget not to rub your eyes while handling them!

Quesadillas with Tomato Salsa

Serves 2–4

This is basically an excellent, fast, easy cheese sandwich with a bit of a kick. This recipe would serve 1 for a main course (I love this for lunch) or it would serve a few people for little bites with drinks before a meal. Or you could serve this as an accompaniment to the main course. These are good served with Tomato Salsa (page 78), Guacamole (page 98), Hot Chilli Sauce (page 80) and Red Onion Raita (page 119).

2 corn or wheat flour tortillas
25 g (1 oz) cheddar, grated or a mixture of cheddar and mozzarella
1 spring onion, sliced (or 1 tbsp of sliced normal onion)
½ green or red chilli, sliced (you can deseed it if you like: just cut the top off at the stalk end, roll the chilli for a second in your hands and then shake out the seeds)

Heat up a frying pan (but don't heat it up too much) and place the tortilla on the hot pan. Sprinkle the grated cheese over the top, keeping the cheese a little from the edge. Next sprinkle the sliced spring onions and the chilli slices on top and cover with the other tortilla. The cheese will have started melting at this stage, and the tortilla on the bottom should be golden brown. When it is, carefully turn it over, keeping it all intact, then cook until the other side is golden and all the cheese has melted. Transfer to a board or plate and cut in wedges. Serve immediately with Tomato Salsa, Guacamole, Hot Chilli Sauce or Red Onion Raita.

NOTE If you have tortillas in the freezer, it's fine to use them from frozen.

Tomato Salsa

Makes 400 ml (14 fl oz)

4 ripe tomatoes, chopped (in the winter I use cherry tomatoes)
1 tbsp onion or spring onion, chopped
1–2 cloves of garlic, crushed
½–1 chilli, finely chopped (taste a tiny bit of the chilli first, you might
want to use more or less depending on how spicy it is)
1 heaped tbsp chopped coriander
juice of ¼–½ lime (if you don't have lime, lemon will suffice)
salt, pepper and sugar

Mix all the ingredients together and season with salt, pepper and a
pinch of sugar.

NOTE Try not to make this more than 1 hour in advance as the tomatoes go quite soft.

Chilli con Carne

Serves 6

I don't care how out of fashion this is, I love it. Mind you, it's probably
so out of fashion it's cool. However, I do think it's better with cubed
rather than minced meat.

2 tbsp olive oil
700 g (1 lb 9 oz) stewing beef, fat removed and cut into 1–2 cm (½–¾ in)
cubes (pork or lamb can also be used)
1–2 large onions, chopped
5 cloves of garlic, crushed

2 x 400 g (14 oz) tins of tomatoes
2 green peppers, deseeded and sliced
3 green or red chillies, chopped (for this I would leave the seeds in)
1–2 tsp freshly ground cumin
400 g (14 oz) tin kidney beans, drained (keep liquid, if you like) or 225 g
(8 oz) dried red kidney beans, soaked and cooked
salt
1 tsp brown sugar
sour cream, coriander leaves and grated cheddar cheese to garnish
(optional)

Heat the olive oil in a casserole or saucepan. Cook the meat until it changes colour, add the onion and garlic and stir around for a minute. Add the tinned tomatoes, peppers, chopped chillies and a good pinch of salt. Cover with a lid, bring to the boil and simmer for about 1 hour or until the meat is cooked (it should be nice and tender). By the end of the cooking time, the liquid should have reduced to a thick sauce. If it gets too dry during cooking, just add a little more water or liquid from the beans. You can also put this into the oven at 150°C/300°F/gas 2. Finally, add the cumin, kidney beans (and a little of the bean liquid, if you like) and brown sugar. Simmer for a further 10 minutes. Serve with rice, a spoonful of sour cream, some grated cheddar, maybe a taco and some coriander leaves sprinkled on top. It's also great with Tomato Salsa (page 78) and Guacamole (page 98), and if some of your friends like a bit more heat, serve the Hot Chilli Sauce (page 80) too!

NOTE Like so many other stews, this gets even better the next day. It also freezes well.

NOTE If you realise at the end of cooking that you haven't put in enough chilli, just add a dash of Tabasco sauce.

Hot Chilli Sauce

Makes 250 ml (9 fl oz)

5 chillies, deseeded or for seriously hot sauce, leave seeds in
1 large onion, chopped
1 red pepper, deseeded and roughly chopped
2 cloves of garlic

Whiz up all the ingredients in a food processor, then add a good pinch of salt and 1 tbsp of water. This will keep in the fridge for a few days and it also freezes well. Great served with Chilli Con Carne or a curry.

Basmati Rice

Serves 8

This is such a good way of cooking rice – you end up with lovely, light, fluffy rice and you can make it slightly in advance. If I'm cooking this rice to serve with a curry or something like that, I add some whole spices to the water and serve them on top of the bowl of rice, such as a small cinnamon stick and a few whole green cardamom pods.

1 tsp salt
450 g (1 lb) basmati rice
15 g (½ oz) butter (optional)

Fill a large saucepan with water and bring up to the boil. Add the salt and the rice, stir for a second or two and boil on a high heat for 4–5 minutes or until the rice is nearly cooked (you want to still have a tiny bit of bite, otherwise the rice will stick later), then strain. Put the rice into a serving dish, stir in the butter if using, cover with tin foil, a plate or a lid and leave it in a low oven (140°C/275°F/gas 1) for at least 15 minutes (it will sit for up to 30 minutes at 100°C/200°F/gas ⅔. When ready to eat, remove the lid, fluff up the rice and serve.

Rodeo Wraps

Makes 4 wraps

For days after I have made a big pot of chilli, I make these wraps for a quick lunch or a supper in front of the television, and I don't always heat up the chilli. These alone are worth making the chilli for.

4 wheat flour tortillas
2 tbsp crème fraîche, seasoned with salt, pepper and 2 tsp lime or
lemon juice
8 tbsp grated cheddar cheese
2 tbsp chopped coriander
250 ml (9 fl oz) leftover Chilli con Carne (about a ¼ of the recipe on page 78), heated up if you like
4 handfuls (aprox. 75 g/2¾ oz) thinly sliced cos or romaine lettuce (optional)

Place a tortilla on the work surface and spread with ½ tbsp seasoned crème fraîche. Sprinkle over 2 tbsp grated cheddar and ½ tbsp chopped coriander, then place about 3 tbsp of Chilli con Carne and 3 tbsp sliced lettuce in a vertical line. Roll up and cut in half at an angle; that way it looks good on a plate. If you want to eat this on the run, fold up the bottom of the tortilla before you roll it, that way the filling won't fall out of the bottom of the wrap.

Chilli Bread

Makes 6

This is an excellent flatbread (not as thin as a tortilla) and I love it to scoop up some chilli with all the sauces. You could also cut this into wedges and serve a plate of it in the centre of the table, and people could dip it into Tomato Salsa (page 78), Guacamole (page 98), Red Onion Raita (page 119) or Hot Chilli Sauce (page 80). Also try other things in it apart from chilli and coriander, like chopped spring onion and rosemary. It's really good warm (but also good cold) and you can reheat it wrapped in tin foil in a moderate oven.

220 g (7 ½ oz) plain flour
2 tsp baking powder
¾ tsp salt
1 chilli, deseeded and chopped
3 tbsp chopped coriander
3 tbsp sunflower or groundnut oil
150–200 ml (5–7 fl oz) boiling water
more oil, for cooking
sea salt

Place flour, baking powder, salt, chilli and coriander in a bowl. In a separate bowl, mix the 3 tbsp oil and 150 ml (5 fl oz) boiling water and add to the dry ingredients. Stir to combine to a soft dough; you may need more water. Knead with your hands for 2 minutes, using extra flour if it sticks to the board. Wrap dough in a plastic bag or cling film and allow to rest for at least 15 minutes.

Divide the dough into 6 equal pieces and roll each portion on a lightly floured surface until 20 cm (8 in) in diameter. Heat a frying pan over a medium heat and add 2 tbsp oil. Add 1 round bread, cover the pan with a lid or plate and reduce the heat to low. Turn the bread over when it's golden brown underneath, about 3 minutes, then flip over and cook the other side. When the bread is golden on both sides, remove from the pan and drain on kitchen paper. Repeat the process with the remaining 5 rounds of dough. Cut each round into wedges and sprinkle with sea salt.

Tiger Prawns in Sweet Chilli Sauce

Serves 4

If you haven't yet bought yourself a bottle of the ubiquitous sweet chilli sauce, go out and get some now! Also called 'dipping sauce for chicken' it sells everywhere now, though I do favour the Flying Goose brand available from Asian stores and good food shops. Needless to say it's great with chicken, but it also livens up everything from hamburgers and sausages to a cheese sandwich. Try dipping roast potato wedges into it and some crème fraîche – totally addictive. Oh yes, it's also good with these tiger prawns too!

40 tiger prawns
approx. 4 tbsp store-bought sweet chilli sauce

Preheat the grill in the oven. Butterfly the tiger prawns by cutting them in half lengthwise, keeping the tail intact to hold it in one piece (you can peel them if you like, but it's not essential). Toss the sweet chilli sauce with the prawns, about 1 tbsp for every 10 prawns, lay them out cut side down in a single layer on a baking tray and place under the hot grill. Grill until cooked and bubbling, about 4 minutes. Serve with Tomato Salsa (page 78), or dip them into a mixture of sweet chilli sauce and crème fraîche.

Thai Beef Salad

Serves 4 as a main course or 6 as a starter

We make this salad at the cookery school, and when I'm in need of super clean, fresh flavours, this does it for me every time!

2 big, thick sirloin steaks (about 450 g (1 lb) of meat altogether)
3 tbsp soy sauce
2 cloves of garlic, crushed
2 tbsp lime juice
4 small handfuls of assorted lettuce leaves
small handful of mint leaves
small handful of basil leaves
small handful of coriander leaves
½ large or 1 small cucumber, split in 2 lengthwise, seeds scooped out with a spoon and cut into ½ cm (¼ in) thick slices, at an angle

dressing:
2 red chillies, chopped (deseed if you wish)
3 tbsp soy sauce
2 tbsp lime juice
2 tsp palm sugar or brown sugar
2 kaffir lime leaves, finely shredded (if you don't have them leave them out, it'll still taste good)

Mix the soy sauce, crushed garlic and lime juice in a bowl and add the steak to marinate for at least 10 minutes. Preheat a grill pan or a good heavy frying pan. When the pan is really hot, cook the steaks for 3–4 minutes on each side or until cooked to your liking. They shouldn't be cooked more than medium rare. Cover the steak and leave to rest on a plate.

Combine all the ingredients for the dressing. Toss the lettuce, mint, basil, coriander and cucumber slices in a bowl. Sprinkle some dressing over the salad leaves and toss. Arrange on a serving plate. Slice the beef thinly and place on top of the salad and drizzle with the remaining dressing. Serve at once.

Spanish Lemon Ice

Serves 4

This is delicious and light just on its own, or fantastic with the Spanish Almond Cake on page 86. This would be very welcome after lots of chilli!

1 free-range egg, separated
250 ml (9 fl oz) milk
140 g (5 oz) caster sugar
finely grated zest and juice of 1 lemon

Whisk the egg yolk with the milk. Add the sugar, grated zest and juice of the lemon. In a separate bowl, whisk the egg white until stiff and fold into the other ingredients. Freeze in a sorbetiere, or alternatively put into a freezer. If it's in the freezer, remove when it's half frozen and whisk it up or break it up in a food processor, then put it back into the freezer until it's completely frozen. Taking it out of the freezer halfway through prevents it from forming ice crystals.

NOTE This makes the ultimate grown-up slush puppy. Put a scoop of lemon ice into the bottom of a frozen glass and add a shot of plain or citron vodka, a splash of soda water if you like and stir. Serve while still really cold with a twist of lemon peel.

Spanish Almond Cake

Serves 6–8

This is great warm or cold and keeps for ages, probably more than a
week if you didn't keep having a slice! It's so good with a cup of coffee
or tea. It's also delicious with a ¼ tsp of ground cinnamon put in at the
start or the grated rind of 1 lemon or 1 small orange. Also fabulous with
ice cream (like the Spanish Lemon Ice on page 85), poached fruit, etc.

3 eggs, separated
150 g (5½ oz) ground almonds
150 g (5½ oz) caster sugar
1 dessertspoon icing sugar, for dusting at the end

You will also need a 18 cm (7 in) springform cake tin.

Preheat the oven to 180°C/350°F/gas 4. Butter the sides of the springform cake tin and cut a round of greaseproof paper to line the base.
Separate the eggs and put the yolks into a medium bowl. Add 130 g
(4½ oz) of the sugar and beat until slightly pale in colour. Add the
ground almonds and mix to combine. In another bowl whisk the egg
whites until they form soft peaks, then add the remaining 20 g (¾ oz)
of sugar and continue whisking the mixture until it forms stiff peaks
and is nice and glossy. Stir one-third of the whisked egg whites into the
almond mixture, then carefully fold in the rest in two batches, not
knocking out any air. Pour the cake batter into the tin and place in the
centre of the preheated oven for 35 minutes or until a skewer comes
out clean from the centre (too high up in the oven and the top gets too
brown). When cooked, let it sit for a few minutes in the tin, then remove
and cool slightly on a wire rack. Sieve some icing sugar over the top.

Sangria

Serves about 8–20 people!

Sangria is such a party drink. This is my brother-in-law Dodo's version.. Some tweaking of the various quantities of the boozy ingredients may be required to suit different occasions (less for your grandmother, more for mad summer parties – or is it the other way around?). If your mood went a little overboard on the booze, you can always add more wine, fruit and soda, which just makes more! In any case, you'll never have any left over.

3 x 750 ml (1¼ pt) bottles Cabernet Sauvignon (or other full-bodied red wine)
2 large oranges
2 large lemons
2 large peaches, sliced
3 tbsp granulated sugar
125 ml (4 fl oz) brandy or to taste
125 ml (4 fl oz) Grand Marnier, or to taste
50 ml (2 fl oz) gin, or to taste
any other fruit, such as strawberries, grapes, cherries (except melon – too mushy)
750 ml (1¼ pt) bottle soda (fizzy mineral) water

Pour the wine into a big pitcher. Using a peeler, remove the rind from the oranges and lemons and place the fruit in with the wine.

Slice the remaining fruit and add to the pitcher. Put in all the other ingredients (except the strawberries, if using, as they'll go mushy) and stir gently. Taste to adjust. Cover and put in the fridge (out of the reach of children!) for 4 hours or so. Just before serving, add the strawberries. Serve in cooled glasses. Enjoy!

Sunday Brunch

This is one of my favourite times of the week. Everyone is relaxed and good and hungry by 11 or 12 o'clock on a Sunday morning. It is a good time to entertain, letting the children run wild and letting everyone else put their feet up and read the papers. You won't need lunch after this!

Crunchy Nutty Muesli

Makes about 1½ kg (3 lb 5 oz)

This is great with milk or natural yoghurt in the morning. Feel free to substitute some of the ingredients – you could use some rye or barley flakes instead of some of the oat flakes or add chocolate chips, dried cranberries or whatever takes your fancy.

125 g (4½ oz) butter
150 ml (5 fl oz) honey
1 tsp vanilla extract
500 g (1 lb 2 oz) oat flakes
100 g (3½ oz) flaked almonds
100 g (3½ oz) chopped cashew nuts
100 g (3½ oz) desiccated coconut
100 g (3½ oz) pumpkin seeds
100 g (3½ oz) sunflower seeds
200–300 g (7–10½ oz) dried fruit, like chopped dried dates, figs, apricots, raisins or sultanas – I like a mixture

Preheat the oven to 170°C/325°F/gas 3. Place the butter, honey and vanilla in a small saucepan and put on the heat to melt together. Put the remaining ingredients, except the dried fruit, in a large bowl and mix. Add in the melted butter and honey mixture and stir really well to make sure it's evenly combined. Spread the muesli out in a large roasting tray and bake in the oven for 25 minutes or until the nuts and grains are a pale golden brown. Stir it around in the oven every 5 minutes so that it browns evenly. Remove the tray from the oven and leave the muesli in the tray to cool, again stirring every now and then. If you transfer it into a bowl while it's warm, it will go soggy. When it has cooled down add the dried fruit, stir and put into an airtight container to store at room temperature. Keeps well for up to a month.

Pancakes with Rashers and Maple Syrup

Makes about 10 pancakes to serve 3–5 people, depending on how hungry everyone is!

Pancakes are often made with buttermilk and bicarbonate of soda, but I devised this recipe with fresh milk and baking powder one morning when I had no buttermilk, and it works perfectly for me!

150 g (5½ oz) self-raising flour (or cream flour with 1 tsp baking powder)
1–2 tbsp caster sugar
1 egg, lightly beaten
150 ml (5 fl oz) milk
50 g (1¾ oz) butter
10 rashers, cooked until nice and crispy
maple syrup

Sieve the flour (and baking powder, if using cream flour) into a bowl, add the sugar and stir. In a separate bowl, whisk together the egg and milk, make a well in the centre of the dry ingredients, add the liquid and mix just until it comes together. Be careful not to over-stir, as if you do the pancakes will turn out too tough.

Heat a frying pan and turn the heat down to medium low. Put half of the butter into the pan and put tablespoonfuls of the mixture into the pan and cook for about 2 minutes, until bubbles appear on the surface (by this time the bottom should be golden brown). Turn the pancakes over and cook until they feel firm in the centre and the bottoms are golden. Repeat with the rest of the mixture. Serve straight from the pan with the crispy rashers and a good drizzle of maple syrup or some butter, a squeeze of lemon juice and some sugar.

NOTE To make cinnamon pancakes, add 1 tsp freshly ground cinnamon. Divine served just with butter melting over the top.

Cinnamon Toast

Serves 4–6

This is a variation on the classic French Bread or Pain Perdu ('lost bread'), as it's best made with your leftover stale bread.

25 g (1 oz) butter
2 eggs
2 tbsp milk (or cream)
2 tsp freshly ground cinnamon
4–6 slices of white bread (preferably a bit stale)
icing sugar, to dust

Place a frying pan on the heat and melt the butter. Lightly whisk the eggs and milk together and pour through a sieve into a bowl. Add the cinnamon. Dip both sides of the bread into the egg mixture and place on the medium-hot pan. Turn over when lightly browned and cook on the other side. Serve straight from the pan, dusted with icing sugar.

NOTE This is also great without the cinnamon.

Bucks Fizz

Serves 2–10 – depends on who's drinking it!

10 oranges
750 ml (1¼ pt) bottle of good sparkling wine (I wouldn't use an
expensive champagne for this, but use a decent bubbly all the same)

Squeeze the juice from the oranges. Pour enough juice into each
champagne glass to fill one-third of the glass. Then slowly top up with
bubbly, being careful it doesn't overflow. Yummmm...

Mango Mimosas

Serves 4–10

1 x 400 g (14 oz) tin mango purée
750 ml (1¼ pt) bottle of good sparkling wine (I wouldn't use an
expensive champagne for this, but use a decent bubbly all the same)

Prepare as with the Bucks Fizz above, but replace the orange juice with
mango purée. You can buy this in Asian stores (Natco does a good one
in a tin) or a French version in good food shops.

30 Day Muffins

Makes 15–20 muffins

Yes, this raw muffin mixture actually keeps in the fridge for 30 days.
In fact, it gets even better as it sits! Make up a batch and cook a few
muffins every day for a month. The longer it sits in the fridge, the drier
it gets, so you could add a tiny bit of water into the mix. This is the
basic recipe, but you can replace the chopped dates and raisins with
grated carrots, grated courgettes or chocolate chips with or without
a bit of grated orange rind.

2 eggs
225 g (8 oz) dark brown sugar
500 ml (18 fl oz) milk
1 tsp vanilla extract
120 ml (4 fl oz) sunflower oil
140 g (5 oz) chopped dates
110 g (4 oz) raisins
2½ rounded tsp bread soda
½ tsp salt
370 g (13 oz) plain flour
110 g (4 oz) bran

Preheat the oven to 180°C/350°F/gas 4. Whisk the eggs and sugar together,
then add the milk and vanilla. Mix well, then add the sunflower oil, dates
and raisins. In a separate bowl, sieve the bread soda and salt with the
flour, add the bran and stir into the wet mixture. Mix again and cover
tightly until needed. Stir the mixture before using. Put muffin cases
into the muffin tin (or paper cases into bun cases) and fill three-quarters
full. Cook for 15–20 minutes or until set and golden. Cool on a wire rack.

Scrambled Eggs with Smoked Salmon

Serves 2

Good scrambled eggs hardly need anything added to them, but sometimes these are nice for a change, for brunch or for supper on the sofa.

4 free-range eggs, best quality possible
4 tbsp milk (a little cream mixed with the milk is, of course, divine!)
salt and pepper
15 g (½ oz) butter
50–75 g (1¾–2¾ oz) smoked salmon, chopped (the trimmings are perfect)
1 tsp chopped chives or parsley (optional)

Break the eggs into a bowl, add the milk and some salt (not too much,
as the smoked salmon can be salty) and pepper and whisk for about
10 seconds. Put the butter into a cold saucepan, add the egg mixture
and stir continuously with a wooden spoon over a low heat until the
mixture looks scrambled, but still soft and creamy. Stir in the smoked
salmon and chives or parsley, taste for salt and pepper and serve.

Scrambled Eggs with Bacon and Parmesan

Serves 2

4 free-range eggs, best quality possible
4 tbsp milk (a little cream mixed with the milk is really good)
salt and pepper
15 g (½ oz) butter
50 g (1¾ oz) bacon, cut into lardons and fried in 1 tbsp olive oil until crisp
25 g (1 oz) parmesan cheese, grated

Make the scrambled eggs as above, but instead of adding salmon, add
the crispy bacon lardons and the grated parmesan just before serving.

Tropical Fruits with Honey and Lime Juice

Serves 2–6

Use whatever good tropical fruits you can find for this. It's best served soon after it has been made.

1 mango, peeled and cut into slices or dice
1 peach or nectarine, cut into slices
1 passion fruit, cut in half and seeds scooped out
1 banana, cut into slices at an angle
1 kiwi, peeled and cut into slices
juice of 2 limes (or 1 lemon)
1–2 tbsp honey

Put all the prepared fruit into a bowl, mix the lime juice and honey together and pour over the fruit, tossing carefully. Serve.

NOTE Of course this is a fantastic dessert too. You could also add 1 tbsp of chopped mint.

NOTE If you have any of this left over, whiz it up with some yoghurt to make a fab smoothie.

Mango and Banana Smoothie

Makes 550 ml (19 fl oz), serves 3–4

What a healthy way to start the day!

1 ripe mango, peeled, stone removed and flesh roughly chopped
2 bananas, peeled
200 ml (7 fl oz) natural yoghurt
1 tbsp lime/lemon juice
1 tbsp honey (optional)
200 ml (7 fl oz) ice (optional)

Put all the ingredients (including the ice, if using) into a blender and whiz up. Taste for lime juice and honey and serve.

Good Coffee with Hot Milk

Makes 6 cups

I love drinking coffee with hot milk out of a big wide cup or a bowl. I make the coffee in a jug. Scald the chosen jug with boiling water, swirl it around, then pour out. Put about 3–4 heaped dessertspoons of freshly ground coffee in a litre-capacity jug, bring the kettle up to the boil again, and wait for the water to stop boiling (takes about 30 seconds and is worth waiting for – if the water is actually boiling, it slightly burns the coffee), then pour on top of the coffee in the jug, stir and wait for 3 or 4 minutes for it to brew. Then pour through a coffee strainer (small sieve) into your mug and half fill with the coffee. Top up with hot milk.

Boys' Lunch

I have called this chapter Boys' Lunch (but let's not be sexist: I would enjoy eating this too) because there are lots of good things here for eating in front of the television while watching the Formula 1 Grand Prix, an international rugby or football match or indeed, whatever you like! No girly salads here! To cook something like this for a man in your life, be it boyfriend, husband, brother or father, I recommend demanding a girls' lunch at home or at your favourite restaurant in return. (Maybe do that first to be sure of a fair deal!)

Tortilla Chips and Guacamole

Serves 6–8

8 wheat or corn tortillas, each cut into 8 wedges
¼ tsp cayenne pepper (optional)
25 g (1 oz) parmesan cheese, grated (optional)
sea salt

Heat up a deep fryer full of oil. When the oil is hot drop in the tortilla wedges and deep fry until pale golden brown. Meanwhile, mix the cayenne with the grated cheese, if using. Take the tortillas out of the oil, and while they're still wet with oil, sprinkle over the cheese and cayenne or just sprinkle over some sea salt. Delicious on their own or dipped into Guacamole, Tomato Salsa (page 78) or Red Onion Raita (page 119), or Sweet Chilli Sauce and creme fraîche.

Guacamole

Serves 6–8

2 ripe avocadoes, peeled and stone removed
2 cloves of garlic, crushed
2 tbsp olive oil (optional)
2 tbsp coriander or parsley, chopped
sea salt and pepper
juice of ½ lime or lemon

Mash the avocado flesh, add all the other ingredients and lime or lemon juice to taste. Put the guacamole into a bowl and place a sheet of cling film on the surface to prevent it going brown. Keep until needed.

Steak Sandwich

Serves 4

2 sirloin steaks, 2.5 cm (1 in) thick
1 clove of garlic, peeled and cut in half
freshly ground black pepper
olive oil
2 demi baguettes (or 1 baguette cut in half)
Horseradish Mayonnaise (page 100) or cold leftover Béarnaise sauce
(page 162)
2 handfuls of rocket leaves

Cut the excess fat off the steaks. Rub both sides of the meat with the
cut clove of garlic, sprinkle with roughly ground black pepper and
drizzle with enough olive oil to coat. Cover and let it sit for 10 minutes
(or put in the fridge for longer).

Meanwhile, make your Horseradish Mayonnaise if it isn't already made.
Heat up a heavy frying pan or grill pan. When smoking hot put the
steaks on and cook for about 5 minutes on each side, depending on
how you like the steak cooked. Don't forget to turn the heat down a
little if the steak is blackening too much! Take the steaks off the pan
and let them rest for 5 minutes in a warm oven while you fetch your
other ingredients. Split the baguette open with a bread knife leaving
one side intact. Slice the steak thinly and put into the baguette with
rocket leaves, sea salt, pepper and a good lashing of Horseradish
Mayonnaise. Eat immediately!

Horseradish Mayonnaise

Makes enough for 6 steak sandwiches

1 x recipe basic mayonnaise, about 300 ml (10 fl oz) (see recipe on page 105)
2–3 tbsp Dijon mustard – yes, really!
1 tbsp caster sugar
1 tsp chopped parsley
2 tsp chopped tarragon
1½ –2 tbsp peeled and finely grated fresh horseradish

Make your basic mayonnaise, then whisk in the other ingredients and season to taste.

Cucumber Pickle

Makes 2 litres (½ pt)

Myrtle Allen started making this in Ballymaloe over 30 years ago. Not only is it good in burgers and all kinds of sandwiches, but it's wonderful with cold sliced meats, smoked fish and transforms a humble hard boiled egg and a chunk of cheddar into a feast. It's a pickle, so even though it will lose its vibrant green colour, it will keep for weeks and weeks.

900 g (2 lb) cucumbers, unpeeled and thinly sliced
3 small onions, thinly sliced
350 g (12 oz) sugar
1 tbsp salt
225 ml (8 fl oz) cider vinegar or white wine vinegar

Mix the cucumber and onion in a large bowl. Add the sugar, salt and vinegar and mix well to combine. Make 1 hour ahead of when you want to use it, if possible.

Chips

Serves 4

enough oil to fill your deep fat fryer (this varies from fryer to fryer)
6 potatoes
salt and pepper

Heat the oil in a deep fryer to about 180°C/350°F/gas 4. If you want buffalo chips, then keep the skins on the potatoes and just scrub them very well. Otherwise peel the potatoes. Cut the potatoes into skinny or fat chips – just remember they should be consistent in size. Make sure the raw chips are completely dry before they go into the deep fryer and don't cook too many at a time. Drop them into the fryer and cook until they are just soft, then drain. When you're ready to eat the chips, increase the heat to 190°C/375°F/gas 5. Put the chips back in and cook until golden and crisp. Sprinkle with salt and serve straight away. Cooking them twice like I do here gives you a really good, crisp chip. If for any reason you do have to keep the chips warm in the oven for a few minutes, make sure that you don't cover them, as they'll go soggy if you do.

NOTE If you don't want to deep fry, try Spicy Potato Wedges (page 47).

Homemade Burgers

Makes 4 good-sized burgers

10 g (¹/₂ oz) butter
75 g (2¾ oz) onion, finely chopped
450 g (1 lb) minced beef – make sure the meat has a bit of fat in it, if not
the burgers will be very dry when cooked
¹/₂ tsp chopped thyme
1 tsp chopped parsley
1 egg, beaten
salt and pepper
olive oil

to serve:
ciabatta bread
lettuce leaves
mayonnaise mixed with Ballymaloe Country Relish
Cucumber Pickle (page 100)

Melt the butter in a small saucepan. Add the onion and sweat over a gentle heat until the onion is soft and pale golden. Take off the heat and leave to get cold. Meanwhile, mix the mince with the herbs and egg and season with salt and pepper. Add the cooled onions and mix. Fry a tiny bit of the mixture in the frying pan to taste it and check for seasoning. Then shape the remaining mixture into hamburger patties and cook on the frying pan with a little olive oil on a medium heat. Turn over halfway through cook-ing. You might need to turn the heat down so as not to burn the burgers.

If you're cooking a couple batches of burgers, clean the pan between batches. While the burgers are cooking, split the ciabatta horizontally and toast under the grill. Then put a lettuce leaf in the bread, some mayonnaise with relish and some Cucumber Pickle. Pop the hot cooked burger inside and eat.

NOTE When shaping the burgers, make sure that they aren't too thick. If they are they will take too long to cook on the inside and may get too charred on the outside.

NOTE If you like you can brown the burgers on both sides on the pan, then transfer into a moderate oven (180°C/350°F/gas 4) until they're cooked. If you want them well cooked they should feel firm in the centre.

NOTE Don't be afraid to experiment with the flavouring here. Beef burgers are delicious with some chopped chilli and coriander instead of the parsley and thyme, or try adding some cayenne pepper, ground cumin and coriander to burgers made with minced lamb. These spicy burgers would be great served with some sweet chilli sauce, which you can buy in stores. In fact, you can even put some sweet chilli sauce (about 1 tbsp) and 1 deseeded and chopped fresh chilli into the raw burger mixture instead of herbs. The possibilities are endless!

Spicy Lamb Burgers

Makes 4 good-sized burgers

*450 g (1 lb) minced lamb – make sure the meat has a bit of fat in it, if
not the burgers will be very dry when cooked*
1 tsp freshly ground cumin
1 tsp freshly ground coriander seeds
¼ tsp freshly ground cinnamon
2 cloves of garlic, crushed
1 egg, beaten
salt and pepper
olive oil

Prepare as on page 102 for the beef burgers. Serve in toasted ciabatta
or warm pitta breads with some sliced tomatoes and fresh coriander.

NOTE I prefer the intense flavour of freshly ground spices. Toasting
the seeds first gives them a nutty flavour and makes them easier to
grind, but be careful not to burn them. I toast them using a dry frying
pan on the hob on a medium to high heat until they turn a shade or
two darker. If you do not have a pestle and mortar, allow the seeds to
cool before putting them in a plastic bag and crushing them with a
rolling pin. Tumeric, cayenne pepper and ginger should be bought in
their ground form.

Mayonnaise

Makes 300 ml (10 fl oz)

2 egg yolks (use leftover egg whites for meringues, either chocolate
or plain)
pinch of salt
½ tsp Dijon mustard
1 dessertspoon white wine vinegar
225 ml (8 fl oz) oil – I like to use 200 ml (7 fl oz) sunflower oil and 25 ml
(1 fl oz) olive oil

Put the egg yolks into a glass bowl. Add the salt, mustard and vinegar
and mix. Gradually add the oil drop by drop, whisking all the time. You
should start to see the mixture thickening. Keep adding the oil as you
whisk until there is no more oil left. Season to taste.

NOTE I often make this with an electric hand blender with the whisk
attachment.

NOTE Homemade mayonnaise lasts for longer than people think, easily
up to a week.

NOTE Mayonnaise is such a fantastic basic sauce. Try adding 3–4 cloves
of crushed garlic and some chopped parsley for garlic mayonnaise, or add
1 tbsp of Ballymaloe Country Relish to make a good sauce for burgers,
steak sandwiches, chicken, etc. Or add more mustard, grated fresh
horseradish and sugar to make Horseradish Mayonnaise (see page 100),
which is excellent with beef and smoked fish. A spoonful of sweet chilli
sauce is a good mix too. The list is endless.

Chicken Wings

Serves 4-6

40 chicken wings
50 ml (2 fl oz) sweet chilli sauce
30 ml (1 fl oz) soy sauce
4 tbsp fresh coriander
2-4 tbsp sesame seeds (optional)

I remove the wing tip first and discard, or else save for stock. Then divide the two joints. For a really fast sauce, toss the wings in enough sweet chilli sauce to coat, then place them in a single layer on a baking tray and cook at 200°C/400°F/gas 6 for 25 minutes. Take them out of the oven and add another good drizzle of sweet chilli sauce and a small drizzle of soy sauce. Give them a little toss and put them back in the oven for another 5-10 minutes or until cooked. Take out of the oven, scatter fresh coriander leaves over the top and serve.

NOTE You could scatter some toasted sesame seeds over them too when they are cooked.

Chinese Ribs

Serves 6–8

I used to use mirin (in place of the wine) and rice vinegar (in place of cider vinegar), but sometimes I wasn't able to get these ingredients and had to work out an alternative. It may sound sacrilegious, but it works perfectly for me.

200 ml (7 fl oz) soy sauce
50 ml (2 fl oz) cider vinegar or red wine vinegar
100 ml (3½ fl oz) white wine
1 generous tbsp hoisin sauce
1 tbsp sesame oil
4 cloves of garlic, crushed
2 tbsp grated ginger
1 tsp ground cinnamon
2 kg (4½ lb) pork spare ribs, cut into portions

Combine all ingredients except the meat and pour over the pork. Leave to marinate for 2 or 3 hours if possible, or you could leave it overnight if you like.

Preheat the oven to 200°C/400°F/gas 6. Place the ribs in a single layer in 2 roasting trays with all the marinade. Cover the trays with tin foil and place in the oven for about 1-1½ hours (or until the pork is nice and tender). Remove the tin foil after 45 minutes and baste the meat every 5 or 10 minutes. When the pork is tender and glazed, remove from the oven, chop into portions and don't forget the finger bowls and lots of napkins!

NOTE If you want the ribs to have lots of lovely juice to mop up with some cooked rice, don't remove the tin foil during cooking.

NOTE These are delicious cooked on the barbeque. Just remove from the marinade before cooking.

Chocolate Sundaes

Serves 2

2 scoops of good vanilla ice cream
2 scoops of good chocolate ice cream
1 banana, sliced
2 tbsp Chocolate Sauce (see recipe on page 109)
2 tbsp Toffee Sauce (see recipe on page 109)
2 tbsp toasted and chopped hazelnuts, walnuts or pecans
2 tbsp whipped cream (optional)

Take 2 sundae glasses and put 1 scoop of vanilla ice cream, 1 scoop of chocolate ice cream and half a sliced banana into each. Drizzle each with 1 tbsp of hot Chocolate Sauce and 1 tbsp of hot Toffee Sauce. Sprinkle each with 1 tbsp of the nuts and finish off with 1 tbsp of whipped cream.

Black Velvets

Serves 4

4 cans of draft Guinness
750 ml (1¼ pt) bottle of decent sparkling wine – not your best champagne, but drinkable nonetheless

By rights, Black Velvets should be served quite elegantly in a champagne flute, made up of half sparkling wine and half Guinness. But apparently for a boys' lunch in front of the match/race, the best way to drink them is out of a pint glass (surprise, surprise!) made up with one-quarter sparkling wine and three-quarters Guinness in each glass. What can I say?

Chocolate Sauce

Makes 175 ml (6 fl oz)

Do try to use a good-quality chocolate for this, something with at least 50 per cent cocoa solids. It will keep for weeks in the fridge.

110 g (4 oz) dark chocolate
25 g (1 oz) butter
30–50 ml (1–2 fl oz) water
1 tsp vanilla extract or a couple tablespoonfuls of rum, brandy or Grand Marnier (optional)
1 tsp grated orange rind (optional)

Place the chocolate, butter and water in a small saucepan and very gently melt it, stirring regularly. Do not allow it to boil. If using, add vanilla or liqueur and orange rind.

Toffee Sauce

Makes 500 ml (18 fl oz)

This is the best recipe, and it keeps for weeks, even months, in the fridge!

275 g (9½ oz) golden syrup
175 g (6 oz) brown sugar
110 g (4 oz) butter
110 g (4 oz) sugar
225 ml (8 fl oz) cream
½ tsp vanilla extract

Put all the ingredients into a saucepan on high heat and boil for about 4 or 5 minutes, stirring regularly, until it's smooth.

Vegetarian Food for Everyone

There are times when we are faced with the dilemma of what to serve to our meat-loving friends when our vegetarian friends are also there. I adore meat, though when it isn't there, I don't miss it. Here are some of my favourite vegetarian recipes.

Spiced Toasted Nuts and Seeds

*a selection of nuts and seeds, such as hazelnuts, skinned almonds,
pistachios, cashews, sunflower seeds, pumpkin seeds – allow 1 handful
per person*

For every handful of nuts or seeds, you'll need:
½ tsp Chinese five-spice powder
¼ tsp dried chilli flakes
¼ tsp sea salt

Heat a frying pan until fairly hot and put in your chosen nuts and
seeds. Stirring them with a wooden spoon, toast them until they start
to turn golden. Add the Chinese five-spice powder, chilli flakes and salt,
continuing to toast for another 30 seconds or so until they are browned
and aromatic. Serve either hot or cold.

NOTE I don't usually add oil into the pan before the nuts, but you can
if you like – about 1 tbsp will do.

NOTE Instead of the five-spice, chilli and salt, you could simply douse
the toasted nuts and seeds with 2–3 tbsp soy sauce when they come
out of the pan. Also very simple and totally addictive!

Onion Bhajis with Tomato and Chilli Sauce

Serves 4 as a starter

I sometimes serve these with Tomato Salsa (page 78), which is good and light, instead of the Tomato and Chilli Sauce.

110 g (4 oz) plain flour
a good pinch of salt
2 tsp baking powder
1 tsp chilli powder
2 eggs, beaten
150 ml (5 fl oz) water
4 onions, thinly sliced
2 tbsp chopped chives
oil for deep frying

First make the Tomato and Chilli Sauce (page 113). Then sieve the flour, salt, baking powder and chilli powder into a bowl. Make a well in the centre, add the eggs and water and whisk into the flour to make a smooth batter. Mix in the onions and chives. Season with salt and pepper.

Just before serving, heat the oil to about 170°C/325°F/gas 3. These can be shallow fried in 4–6 tablespoons of sunflower oil or in a deep fryer. Either way you must turn them over halfway through cooking. Pop in dessertspoonfuls of the onion batter and fry for about 5 minutes on each side, until golden, then drain on kitchen paper. Serve with the Tomato and Chilli Sauce.

Tomato and Chilli Sauce

Makes 250 ml (9 fl oz)

2–3 green chillies (depending on size and taste), deseeded and chopped
2 tbsp water
1 clove of garlic, crushed
1 tbsp white wine vinegar
1 dessertspoon caster sugar
1 dessertspoon brown sugar
½ of a 400 g (14 oz) tin chopped tomatoes
salt and pepper

Put all the ingredients into a small saucepan and simmer with the lid off for 10 minutes, until reduced by half. Keeps for a week or two.

Mustard and Honey Salad Dressing

Makes 200 ml (7 fl oz)

150 ml (5 fl oz) olive oil
30–50 ml (1–2 fl oz) balsamic vinegar
1 large clove of garlic, crushed
1 tsp of grainy mustard with honey (I use Lakeshore)
1 tsp honey
sea salt and freshly ground black pepper

Mix everything together and taste – it may need more salt, vinegar, etc. Dipping a lettuce leaf into it to taste is a good way of judging the seasoning and flavour.

Rocket, Pear and Blue Cheese Salad

Serves 4 as a starter

This couldn't be more simple, but it's great for a dinner party, served on big plates with freshly grilled, crusty white bread drizzled with some leftover dressing.

4 handfuls of rocket leaves
2 good pears, unpeeled and thinly sliced
200 g (7 oz) good ripe blue cheese, broken up with your hands into big, rough pieces (about 3 cm/1 in)
50 ml (2 fl oz) olive oil
1 tbsp balsamic vinegar
sea salt and freshly ground black pepper

Divide the rocket leaves between 4 plates, or place on 1 large plate. Arrange the sliced pears and blue cheese on top of the rocket. Mix the olive oil and balsamic vinegar, season with sea salt and pepper and drizzle some dressing over the top.

Courgette Frittata

Serves 6

A frittata is an Italian omelette, much like a Spanish tortilla (see page 20).

500 g (1 lb 2 oz) courgette, unpeeled (try to choose smallish ones –
approx. 5)
15 g (½ oz) butter
1 tbsp olive oil
6 eggs
150 ml (5 fl oz) cream
100 g (3½ oz) grated Gruyère or parmesan cheese
3 cloves of garlic, crushed
1 tbsp torn basil
½ tbsp chopped chives
salt and pepper

Grate one side of the courgette, then as soon as you get down to the seeds, turn to the other side and continue to grate, leaving out the seedy centre. Heat a frying pan, add the butter and oil and cook the courgette until just soft but not coloured, about 2 minutes. In a big bowl, whisk the eggs, add the remaining ingredients and season with salt and pepper to taste. Slightly heat a frying pan and add 3 tbsp olive oil. Swirl it around to coat the pan, then pour in the egg mixture. Cook on a low heat until it's golden underneath, about 10 minutes, then place under a hot grill to set the top. Serve with a green salad with the dressing on page 113.

NOTE You could also make individual frittatas by brushing a muffin tin with olive oil and then filling each cup three-quarters full. Pop into the oven heated to 180°C/350°F/gas 4 for 20–25 minutes or until firm in the centre. These are good to bring along on a picnic, as they're still tasty served cold. Made this way, you should get 20 individual frittatas.

Gratin of Potatoes and Leeks with Garlic and Thyme

Serves 6

I love a bowl of this on a cold winter's night. Serve it on its own or as an accompaniment to roast lamb, chicken or beef.

50 g (1¾ oz) butter
300 g (10½ oz) leeks, sliced ½ cm (¼ in) thick
3 cloves of garlic, crushed or grated
2 tsp chopped thyme or rosemary
1 kg (2¼ lb) potatoes, peeled and sliced ½ cm (¼ in) thick
350 ml (12 fl oz) cream
salt and pepper

Preheat the oven to 180°C/350°F/gas 4. In a pan, melt the butter, add the sliced leeks, garlic and chopped thyme, cover with a butter wrapper or a disc of greaseproof paper and a lid and cook on a low heat until just soft, about 5 minutes. Meanwhile, place the potato slices into a pot of boiling water, cook for 3 minutes and drain. Lightly butter a large gratin dish or individual dishes and add a layer of overlapping potato slices. Season the potatoes and cover with the leeks and all the juices, then add the final layer of potato slices and season again. Pour over the cream and bake in the oven for 45–55 minutes (or less for smaller dishes) or until bubbly and golden.

Dal with Chilli and Garam Masala Mash

Serves 4

This has to be one of my favourite comfort foods. I love it served with this Chilli and Garam Masala Mash. Chilli Bread (page 82) is also excellent with this, particularly if you're leaving out the mash.

25 g (1 oz) butter
2 tbsp sunflower oil
1 onion, chopped
2 cloves of garlic, crushed
1 small red chilli, deseeded and chopped
1 small pinch asafoetida (optional), used mainly for its digestive properties
225 g (8 oz) red lentils
750 ml (1¼ pt) or more water
2 tsp ground cumin seeds
½ tsp ground turmeric
1 tbsp chopped coriander

Melt the butter in a saucepan with the oil. Add the onions, garlic, chilli, asafoetida (if using) and a pinch of salt and cook on a low heat until the onions are soft. Then add the lentils and stir around for a few seconds. Add one-quarter of the water and simmer slowly until the water has reduced and been absorbed into the lentils. Then add some more water, cook again and repeat the process until the lentils are cooked and the water has all been absorbed into the dal. Add the cumin to taste, the turmeric, chopped coriander and another pinch of salt if it needs it. This can be reheated over a low flame.

NOTE Asafoetida is used mainly for its digestive properties as it helps to combat flatulence! It is normally found in ground form and can be bought from Asian and health food shops. Although it has a strong smell its flavour is slight and truffle-like.

Chilli and Garam Masala Mash

Serves 6

1 kg (2¼ lbs) potatoes, scrubbed, in their skins
3–6 cloves of garlic, peeled
50 g (1¾ oz) butter
150–300 ml (5–10 fl oz) boiling milk
1 red chilli, deseeded and chopped (or more if you like)
1–1½ tsp garam masala
1–2 tbsp chopped coriander

Put the scrubbed potatoes into a saucepan, fill up with water and add a good pinch of salt. Bring up to the boil. After 5 minutes of boiling pour off most of the water, leaving about 3 cm (1 in) of water in the bottom, and continue cooking on a low heat, checking every so often that the water hasn't evaporated and leaving you with burned potatoes! 20 minutes after the potatoes have gone in to cook, put the whole garlic cloves into the saucepan; they should be cooked by the time the potatoes are. When they're all cooked, peel the potatoes and mash the potatoes and garlic together. Add the butter, a little boiling milk, the chilli, garam masala, chopped coriander and some salt. Check for seasoning and add more milk or spices as required. Serve with the dal and a bowl of Red Onion Raita (page 119) or Cucumber Raita (page 45) and scatter coriander leaves over the top.

NOTE Make sure the potatoes are completely mashed before adding the boiling milk, otherwise they'll stay lumpy.

NOTE You can buy garam masala ready made. There are many different recipes for making it, but this is one that I normally use. In a food processor, whiz up 2 tsp of green cardamom seeds, ½ tsp each of cumin seeds, cloves, black peppercorns, nutmeg and a 2 cm (¾ in) piece of cinnamon until fine. Keep any leftovers in an airtight container.

  Vegetarian Food for Everyone

Red Onion Raita

Serves 6

150 ml (5 fl oz) natural yoghurt
1 large red onion, finely chopped
*1 tsp cumin seeds, toasted on a dry frying pan and ground (toasting gives
the cumin a wonderful nutty flavour and also makes it easier to crush)*
1 clove of garlic, crushed or finely grated
1 small green or red chilli, deseeded and chopped
2 tbsp chopped coriander
½ tsp sugar
juice of ¼–½ lemon
salt to taste

Mix all the ingredients together, taste and add more seasoning or
spices if you like. Pour into a bowl. If you want to make this more than
a couple of hours in advance, place the chopped onions in a sieve, wash
under water and drain. This prevents the onion from developing a
strong, oxidising flavour. You can also add chopped tomatoes to this.

Falafel in Warm Pitta Bread

Makes 4 patties, serves 2

This Middle Eastern street food is hard to beat: spiced chickpea fritters served in warm pitta bread with cucumber, tomato, natural yoghurt and a drizzle of tahini.

400 g (14 oz) tin of chickpeas, drained
2–3 cloves of garlic, crushed or grated
1 small onion, chopped
1 tsp ground coriander
1 tsp toasted and ground cumin
1 tbsp chopped parsley
1 tbsp plain flour

to serve:
2 pitta breads
¼ cucumber, sliced
2 large tomatoes, sliced and seasoned with salt, pepper and a pinch of sugar
4 tbsp natural yoghurt
2 tbsp tahini paste (optional)

To make the falafel, whiz up the chickpeas, garlic, onion, spices and parsley in a food processor until just smooth. Empty into a bowl, add in the flour and season to taste. It will taste quite strong, but don't worry, it needs to be since it will mellow when it's cooked.

Flour your hands and shape the mixture into 4 patties and fry them in a little oil until golden on both sides (about 3–4 minutes on a medium to low heat). While they're cooking heat up the pittas, then split them open and pop 2 falafels into each, followed by slices of cucumber and the seasoned tomato slices. Spoon over the yoghurt and tahini, if using. Eat immediately!

Vegetarian Food for Everyone

Mangoes and Bananas in Lime Syrup

Serves 4

Delicious served with greek yoghurt, whipped cream, crème fraîche, vanilla ice cream or the Coconut and Lime Ice (page 122). It's amazing for breakfast too (if there's any left over!).

110 g (4 oz) sugar
125 ml (4 fl oz) water
1 ripe mango
2 bananas
grated zest and juice of 1–2 limes

Put the sugar and water into a saucepan and stir over a medium heat to dissolve the sugar. Bring up to the boil and simmer for 2 minutes. Let cool. Peel the mango and slice quite thinly down to the stone. Slice the banana and put the fruit into a bowl with the cool syrup. Add the zest and juice of the lime, chill and serve.

NOTE Nectarines and peaches are really good in this too instead of the mango or the bananas.

Coconut and Lime Ice

Serves 6

You have to try this: it's the best way to end a spicy meal. It's like a mixture between an ice cream and a sorbet. Serve in little glasses or cups on its own or with some of the Mango and Bananas in Lime Syrup (page 121). I love it.

125 g (4½ oz) sugar
125 ml (4 fl oz) water
400 g (14 oz) tin of coconut milk
grated rind and juice of 2 limes

Put the sugar and water into a small saucepan on medium heat, stirring to dissolve the sugar, then boil for 2–3 minutes. Cool completely. When it's cold, whisk in the coconut milk, rind and juice of the limes. Pour the mixture into a container and freeze. When it's semi-frozen, whisk it to break up any ice crystals and quickly put back in the freezer. You can repeat this process again if you want a very smooth ice; I sometimes don't.

NOTE You can even go one step further and take it out of the bowl in which it's freezing and whiz it up in a food processor with 1 slightly beaten egg white, then quickly pop it back in the freezer. This will give you a fantastically smooth ice, as though you've churned it in an ice cream machine, which of course if you have one is the thing to use!

Fresh Gingerade

Makes 1¾ litres (3 pt)

225 g (8 oz) sugar
300 ml (10 fl oz) water
6 lemons or 10 limes, juiced
2 tbsp finely grated ginger
¾ –1 litre (1¼–1¾ pt) water

Put the sugar and water into a saucepan, stirring to dissolve the sugar over a medium heat, then bring up to the boil and simmer for 2 minutes. Let cool. Mix the lemon or lime juice with the ginger, add most of the cold syrup and top up with water to taste. Add the rest of the syrup if you like. Add ice and serve.

NOTE Roll the limes under your hand on the work surface to soften them – it makes juicing them easier.

Simple Comfort Food

*Sometimes we need food that is soothing, warming
and comforting. It might be a big bowl of soup, a hearty
stew or a sweet hot chocolate.*

Oriental Broth

Serves 4 as a starter, or 2 as a supper in itself

This is what my sister, Simone, calls 'clean' food. If I'm in need of a bit of detox comfort food, this is the kind of thing that I have a big steaming bowl of before an early night in bed!

500 ml (18 fl oz) chicken or vegetable stock
2 x 2 cm (¾ in) pieces of fresh ginger, bashed slightly with a rolling pin
½ chilli, deseeded and chopped
1 spring onion, sliced thinly at an angle
1 tsp dark brown sugar
½ tbsp nam pla (Thai fish sauce)
juice of ½ lime
1 tbsp chopped coriander
1 tbsp chopped mint

Boil the stock and ginger for 3 minutes, add the rest of the ingredients except for the herbs and simmer for 1 minute. Take off the heat, add the herbs and serve.

NOTE If you feel like something a little more substantial, add 2 thinly sliced chicken breasts to the stock and ginger at the start and/or 50 g (1¾ oz) thin cellophane (mung bean) noodles or thin rice noodles which have been soaked in boiling water for 5 minutes or until soft. Put these into the soup bowls and ladle over the soup.

NOTE I sometimes add 2 handfuls of bean sprouts in with the remainder of the ingredients.

Risotto alla Parmigiana

Serves 6–8

Use a high-quality stock for the best risotto.

1½ litre (2¾ pt) light chicken stock (see recipe on page 42)
25 g (1 oz) butter
3 tbsp olive oil
1 onion, finely chopped
500 g (1 lb 2 oz) risotto rice, such as Arborio or Roma Carnaroli
1 glass of white wine (optional)
75 g (2¾ oz) parmesan, freshly grated
sea salt and pepper

Put the stock into a pot and bring to the boil, then reduce the heat and keep it at a simmer. Meanwhile, melt the butter in a large saucepan with the oil, add the onion and some salt and sweat gently until soft. Add the rice and stir around for a minute. Then, if you're using the white wine (which I do if I have some handy), add it in at this stage and let it bubble up and evaporate, which will take a few minutes on a medium heat.

Add a ladleful (about 150 ml/5 fl oz) of the simmering stock and stir continuously. As soon as the liquid is absorbed, add another ladleful. Continue to cook, stirring continuously over a medium heat, and repeat the process with the stock until the rice is cooked and is loose and creamy in consistency, which should take about 25 minutes. When you're happy with the texture (you might need to add more stock), stir in the grated parmesan cheese and check for seasoning. Serve.

NOTE There are so many variations of risotto. To make Risotto al Funghi, add in about 10 g (½ oz) dried mushrooms, such as cepes, porcini or boletus, that you've covered in hot water to soften (save the

Simple Comfort Food

soaking water and use it in place of some of the stock). Add the mushrooms about 10 minutes before the end of cooking. Alternatively, you could add some cooked asparagus spears and mange tout at the end of the cooking. Or you could even replace the white wine with red wine for a wonderfully robust winter risotto.

Italian White Bean Soup with Rosemary

Serves 4–6

If you are using a tin of cooked beans, as I normally do, this is a really fast soup to whip up on a cold winter day.

2–3 tbsp olive oil
1 onion, chopped, (about 150 g / 5¹/₂ oz)
2 cloves of garlic, chopped
1 x 400 g (14 oz) tin of butter beans or cannelini beans, keeping all the liquid
350 ml (12 fl oz) vegetable or chicken stock
2 tsp chopped rosemary

Put the olive oil in a saucepan, add the onion and garlic, season with salt and pepper and cook over a low heat until the onion is completely cooked, but not coloured. Add the beans and their liquid and most of the stock and boil for 5 minutes, then add the chopped rosemary and liquidise, adding more stock if required. Season to taste.

NOTE This is also great with a teaspoon of pesto (basil or parsley) or Herb and Olive Oil Dip instead of the chopped rosemary. Drizzle it over each bowl when you are serving it.

NOTE I sometimes add cooked slices of chorizo sausage into a bowl of this too (like the Potato and Parsnip Soup on page 156).

Italian Beef Stew with Pea and Spring Onion Champ

Serves 6–8

Italy meets Ireland in this gutsy wintertime dish.

1½ kg (3 lb 5 oz) stewing beef, cut into cubes
175 g (6 oz) streaky bacon
3 tbsp olive oil
12 baby onions, peeled
18 button mushrooms, left whole
3 carrots cut into quarters or 12 baby carrots, scrubbed and left whole
salt and pepper
1 tbsp chopped rosemary
1 tbsp chopped thyme
10 cloves of garlic, crushed or grated
425 ml (15 oz) red wine
425 ml (15 oz) chicken or beef stock
roux (see recipe on page 66)
2 tbsp chopped parsley

Brown the beef and bacon in the olive oil in a hot casserole or heavy saucepan. Remove the meat and toss in the onions, mushrooms and carrots, one ingredient at a time, seasoning each time. Place all these ingredients back in the casserole, along with the herbs and garlic. Cover with red wine and stock and simmer for 1 hour or until the meat and vegetables are cooked. When the stew is cooked, remove the meat and vegetables. Bring the remaining liquid to the boil and add 1 tbsp roux. Whisk the mixture until the roux is broken up and the juices have thickened. Allow to boil. Replace the meat and vegetables, and taste for seasoning. Sprinkle with the chopped parsley and serve with Pea and Spring Onion Champ.

Simple Comfort Food

Chicken Wings

Tortilla Chips with Sweet Chilli Sauce and Guacamole

Pan-Toasted Sandwich with Tomato, Chilli and Gubeen Cheese

Crunchy Nutty Muesli

Spiced Nectarines

Chocolate Meringues and Chocolate Cream

Affogato al Caffe

Pea and Spring Onion Champ

Serves 6–8

1½ kg (3 lb 5 oz) potatoes, scrubbed
100 g (3½ oz) butter
500 ml (18 fl oz) milk (or if you want it really rich, use ¾ milk to ¼ cream)
450 g (1 lb) peas
75 g (2¾ oz) spring onions, chopped
4 tbsp chopped parsley
salt and freshly ground pepper

Cook the potatoes in boiling salted water for 5–10 minutes, until tender, then drain three-quarters of the water and continue to cook on a low heat. Avoid stabbing the potatoes with a knife, because if they're floury potatoes they'll break up if you do. When they're cooked, drain all the water off, peel and mash with most of the butter while hot.

Meanwhile, place the milk in a saucepan with the peas and spring onion and boil for 4 or 5 minutes, until cooked. Add the parsley and take off the heat. Add to the potatoes, keeping some of the milk back in case you don't need it all. Season to taste and beat until creamy and smooth, adding more milk if necessary. Serve piping hot with the remaining butter melting in the centre.

Chicken and Bacon Casserole

Serves 4–8

This is simple comfort food, just how it should be. If you like your casserole dish enough, serve the chicken straight from this in the centre of the table.

450 g (1 lb) piece of streaky bacon, cut into 2 cm (¾ in) chunks
4 tbsp olive oil
1 chicken, jointed into 8 pieces
4 medium carrots, peeled and cut into 4 cm (1½ in) chunks, or 12 baby carrots, scrubbed and left whole
10 baby onions, peeled or 4 medium onions, peeled and halved (red onions are good too)
6–8 garlic cloves, peeled
400 ml (14 fl oz) chicken stock or, failing that, water
sprig of thyme, rosemary or sage

Put the bacon into a small saucepan of cold water and bring up to the boil to remove any excess salt. Drain, then dry the bacon on kitchen paper. Heat up a frying pan, add 2 tbsp olive oil and sauté the bacon until golden and crispy. Remove to a casserole, then add the chicken to the pan, adding more oil if necessary. Sauté the chicken for a few minutes until golden, then remove to the casserole. Next, sauté the carrots, onions and garlic for a minute, seasoning with salt and pepper, then add them to the other sautéed ingredients in the casserole. Deglaze the frying pan by adding the stock to the frying pan over a high heat, dissolving all the juices on the bottom. Then pour the stock into the casserole. Add a sprig of thyme, rosemary or sage and put into the oven at 160°C/325°F/gas 3 for about 45 minutes or until cooked. Strain the juices if you like (if you haven't added flour at the start; see note below), spoon any fat off the top and add back in to the stew. Sprinkle with some chopped parsley. Serve with mashed potatoes.

NOTE You could put potatoes on top of this in the casserole, like in the Irish Stew on page 132.

NOTE You could also add 150 ml (5 fl oz) white wine into the stock when you are deglazing the pan.

NOTE If you want the juices to be slightly thick, you could toss the chicken pieces in flour seasoned with a little salt and pepper before you brown them, making sure not to burn them. Or you could thicken the juices with some roux (page 66) at the very end, then pour back into the chicken and vegetables.

Irish Stew

Serves 4–6

There are endless versions of Irish Stew. Some people say you should just have white vegetables in it, some people add 1 or 2 tbsp of pot barley in at the start with the stock.

1–1½ kg (2¼–3 lb 5 oz) gigot chops with bones attached or mutton neck chops
3 tbsp olive oil or 3 tbsp of the lamb or mutton fat that you've put into the hot casserole or saucepan to render down
4 medium carrots, peeled and quartered or 12 baby carrots, scrubbed and left whole
12 baby onions, peeled or 4 medium onions, cut into quarters through the root, which should keep the quarters intact
8 cloves of garlic, peeled (not traditional, but I love garlic in Irish Stew)
15 g (½ oz) butter
salt and pepper
600 ml (1 pt) lamb or chicken stock or water
8–12 potatoes, peeled
sprig of rosemary or a large sprig of thyme
1 tbsp chopped parsley
1 tbsp chopped chives

Cut the chops in half, not taking off the bones. Heat the oil or fat in the casserole until it's very hot and toss the meat in until it's nice and brown. Remove the meat to a plate and cook the carrots, onions and garlic in the hot oil or fat for a couple of minutes, seasoning with salt and pepper while sautéing. Put the meat back in with the vegetables. Add the stock and season again. Put the potatoes on top and simmer gently, either in the oven at 160°C/325°F/gas 3 or on the hob, until the meat is cooked, about 1½ hours, though it may take longer. Pour off the cooking liquid, degrease, season if it needs it and pour back over the stew. Add the herbs and serve.

NOTE If the potatoes are quite small, add them in 20–30 minutes after the stew starts cooking.

NOTE To degrease the juices if you don't have a maisgras, add a couple of ice cubes to the strained liquid. The fat should rise up to the top, spoon it off and discard.

NOTE If you like, you could thicken the juices with some roux (see page 66).

Pan-Toasted Sandwich with Tomato, Chilli and Gubbeen Cheese

Makes 2 sandwiches

This is the ultimate toasted cheese sandwich, and I often alter the ingredients depending on what I have in the fridge. I love the semi-soft, creamy Gubbeen cheese, but you can use any good cheese (though not soft goats' cheese, it runs out of the sandwich when it cooks).

4 tbsp olive oil
¼ red chilli, deseeded and chopped
2 small cloves of garlic, crushed or finely grated
good pinch of sea salt and freshly ground black pepper
2 ripe tomatoes, sliced
4 slices of good white bread
75 g (2¾ oz) Gubbeen cheese, sliced
6 basil leaves, or rocket or watercress
15 g (½ oz) butter

Place 2 tbsp of the olive oil, chopped chilli, garlic, salt and pepper into a bowl and mix. Add the sliced tomatoes and toss gently in the oil. Brush one side of each piece of bread with the chilli and garlic oil from the tomatoes and set 2 of the pieces of bread aside. Place the sliced cheese onto 2 of the pieces of bread, on top of the oil, then the basil leaves on top of that, then the tomatoes, then top with the 2 slices of bread that you set aside, oiled side down. Melt the butter and the remaining 2 tbsp olive oil in a frying pan over a medium heat and add the sandwiches. Cover with a lid or plate and cook until golden brown on one side, turn over and cook on the other side until golden, still covered with a lid or plate. Serve now!

Pan-Toasted Chocolate Sandwich

Makes 2 sandwiches

I could eat these for breakfast, lunch and supper. What more can I say?

4 slices of white bread
soft butter for spreading
50 g (1¾ oz) good-quality dark chocolate, chopped or grated

Spread one side of each piece of bread with butter. Turn 2 of the slices over and sprinkle with the chopped chocolate on the unbuttered side. Top with the other slices of bread, buttered side up. Heat a frying pan over a gentle heat. Add the sandwiches and cook, turning once, until the bread is golden brown on both sides and the chocolate is melting. Serve at once.

Hot Chocolate

Serves 1

When thinking of a drink to put in the comfort food section, hot chocolate kept springing to mind. I don't expect you to drink this after a big bowl of stew, though!

200 ml (7 fl oz) milk
50 g (1¾ oz) good-quality dark chocolate
2 cm (¾ in) piece of cinnamon
1 strip of orange peel (removed with a peeler)

Put everything into a saucepan and slowly heat up, stirring to gently melt the chocolate. Pour into a cup, sit down and grab your favourite book.

Simple Comfort Food

Hot Lemon Puddings

Serves 6

When cooked, these puddings have a layer of lemon sponge sitting on top of a layer of hot lemon curd.

50 g (1¾ oz) butter
2 eggs, separated
200 g (7 oz) sugar
50 g (1¾ oz) plain flour, sieved
finely grated rind and juice of 1 lemon
225 ml (8 fl oz) milk
icing sugar, for dusting

Preheat the oven to 150°C/300°F/gas 2. Cream the butter until very soft, add the egg yolks and sugar and beat together. Add in the sieved flour, the grated rind and juice of the lemon and then the milk. In a separate clean, dry bowl, whisk the 2 egg whites until stiff and then fold into the flour mixture. Pour the custard into 6 ramekins or tea cups and bake in the preheated oven for 25 minutes or until just set. You could also use 1 large pie dish (capacity 1.2 litres/2 pt) for 40 minutes. Cool slightly and dredge icing sugar over the top.

Chocolate Fudge Pudding

Serves 6

I have tried many other versions of Chocolate Fudge Pudding, and in my opinion, this recipe from Darina is unbeatable. Of course, it's best served straight out of the oven, but it's still pretty good the next day, if you can manage to have any left over! Don't overcook this, otherwise you'll lose the fudginess. Amazing served with vanilla ice cream.

150 g (5½ oz) good dark chocolate
150 g (5½ oz) unsalted butter (use salted if you don't have it)
1 tsp vanilla extract
150 ml (5 fl oz) warm water
110 g (4 oz) caster sugar
4 eggs
25 g (1 oz) self-raising flour, sieved
pinch of cream of tarter
icing sugar, to dust

Preheat the oven to 200°C/400°F/gas 6. Very gently melt the chocolate, butter, vanilla, water and sugar in a saucepan on a low heat. Take off the heat, transfer into a bowl and stir until the mixture is smooth. Separate the eggs, whisk the yolks into the chocolate mixture, then fold in the sieved flour. In a separate dry, clean bowl, whisk the egg whites with a pinch of cream of tarter until it forms stiff peaks. Gently fold this into the chocolate mixture and pour into a 1.2 litre (2 pt) pie dish or 6 individual dishes. Place in a bain marie (a pan or roasting tray with about 2 cm (¾ in) of water in it, which protects the pudding from the harsh heat and prevents it drying out). Cook for 10 minutes (for the single dish), then lower the heat to 170°C/325°F/gas 3 and cook for a further 20–30 minutes. If you're cooking individual puddings, then just cook them for 15 minutes at 200°C/400°F/gas 6. The pudding should be firm on top but still fudgy underneath. Cool a little and dredge with icing sugar. Serve with softly whipped cream.

Summer Lunch

Make the most of all the wonderful ingredients that
are in season and really only taste good in summer, like plump
red ripe tomatoes, fresh wild salmon, strawberries, rhubarb and
raspberries. Try a cocktail with a summer feeling, such as the
Rhubarb Mimosa, and you can't fail!

Tomato and Mozzarella Salad with Tapenade Crostini

Serves 6

4 large, ripe tomatoes
sea salt, pepper and sugar
10 basil leaves
2 balls of mozzarella cheese

Preheat the oven to 220°C/425°F/gas 7. Cut the tomatoes into quarters and then in half across the wedge. Season with sea salt, pepper, sugar and some torn basil. Cut the mozzarella cheese into a similar size as the tomatoes and gently toss together. Season to taste. Divide between 6 plates and place a Tapenade Crostini on the side of each plate.

Tapenade

Makes 150 ml (5 fl oz)

110 g (4 oz) stoned black olives
50 g (1¾ oz) anchovy fillets
1 tbsp capers
1 tsp Dijon mustard
1 tsp freshly squeezed lemon juice
pepper
4 tbsp olive oil

In a food processor, whiz up the olives with the anchovies, capers, mustard, lemon juice and pepper. Add the olive oil. Keeps for months in a sterilised jar in the fridge.

Crostini

½ a baguette
olive oil
tapenade

Cut the baguette into 6 slices at an angle and toss in olive oil to coat. Put into the hot oven to toast for about 5 minutes or until pale golden. Take out of the oven and spread thinly with tapenade.

Avocado, Orange and Red Onion Salad

Serves 4

for the dressing:
50 ml (1¾ fl oz) olive oil
1–2 tbsp chopped black olives
1½–2 tbsp sherry vinegar or balsamic vinegar
sea salt and freshly ground black pepper

for the salad:
2 handfuls of rocket leaves
1 large avocado, peeled, stoned and cut into 2 cm (¾ in) chunks
2 oranges, peeled with a knife to remove all the pith and cut into thin slices
½ small red onion, very thinly sliced
2 tbsp sliced basil (lay the leaves on top of each other, roll up like a sausage and slice)

Mix together all the ingredients for the dressing, then season to taste.
Divide the rocket leaves between 4 plates and add the chunks of
avocado, the slices of orange and the slivers of red onion. Drizzle the
dressing over the top and sprinkle with the sliced basil. Serve at once.

Zac's Paella

Serves 10

In Spain this is cooked in and served from a paella pan, a big, wide, shallow pan with handles on either side, which can be bought very cheaply from supermarkets. Use any big, wide saucepan you can find, or pick up one of these pans when next in Spain! This is delicious – it's really worth the effort!

4 tbsp olive oil
110 g (4 oz) butter
4 shallots, sliced
8 cloves of garlic, crushed
24 prawns, peeled
450 g (1 lb) squid, cleaned and cut into rings, plus whole tentacles
400 g (14 oz) paella rice, or Arborio or Roma Carnaroli (risotto rice)
50 ml (2 fl oz) white wine
600 ml (1 pt) light fish stock, simmering in a small saucepan

12 asparagus spears, woody ends removed and cut into 3
450 g (1 lb) peas or mange tout
600 ml (1 pt) vegetable cooking water (see below)
450 g (1 lb) small courgettes, sliced
24 each of mussels and clams, cleaned and debearded (the little tuft of hair-like fibre that sticks out of the opening of the shell)
a good pinch of saffron
juice of 1 lime
4 tbsp chopped parsley and chives
salt and pepper

Melt the olive oil and butter in a very large pan and slowly cook the shallot and garlic until they're soft. Add the prawns and raw squid and cook for 2–3 minutes until they stiffen, remove and set to one side.

Next add the rice and wine to the pan and cook for a few minutes until nearly all the wine has evaporated, stirring regularly. Add a third of the fish stock to the rice and let simmer, still stirring regularly, until it has been absorbed. Repeat this process twice again and let it simmer until the liquid has evaporated and been absorbed by the rice; it's a little like making a risotto.

Meanwhile, cook the asparagus in 600 ml (1 pt) of boiling salted water for about 4 minutes. Add the peas after 2 minutes and finish cooking them together. When they're cooked, drain, but keep the cooking water, and refresh the vegetables under cold running water. Cook the courgettes in a separate frying pan over a high flame with 1 tbsp olive oil, salt and pepper; put to one side when done.

Steam the mussels and clams in a covered pot with 1 tbsp water, until they're wide open. Put aside and strain the juices if there is any sand and discard any that haven't opened. Add the saffron, lime juice and the vegetable liquid to the mussel and clam juices. Add this to the rice 200 ml (7 fl oz) at a time, stirring and letting the rice absorb the last bit before you add the next. You might not need all the liquid – you'll know by the texture of the rice when it's cooked. It should be soft, loose and creamy, the consistency of risotto. When the paella is fully cooked, gently fold the vegetables and shellfish through the rice, season to taste and sprinkle with the chopped parsley and chives. You really need to serve a good green salad with or after this Paella!

NOTE When using mussels and clams, make sure that they're all fresh. They should all be tightly shut; if they aren't, give them a little tap and if they don't close, then throw them out.

Poached Salmon with Hollandaise Sauce

Serves 6

*1½ kg (3 lb 5 oz) piece of salmon, cut into a section, not a salmon steak
or filleted*
salt

Choose a saucepan that will just fit the chunk of salmon you have. Half
fill with measured salted water (using 1 tbsp salt to every 1.2 litre (2
pt) of water), bring to the boil and add the piece of fish. Bring back to
the boil and simmer gently for 20 minutes. Turn off the heat and allow
to sit in the water for a further 5 minutes.

To serve, pull off the skin, and using a fish slice, ease some salmon off
the bone (it won't come off the bone if it isn't cooked) and put it on
the plate. Serve with Hollandaise Sauce, new potatoes, asparagus or
peas and a green salad.

NOTE This will keep in a warm oven, covered, for about 20 minutes.

NOTE You need to allow about 100–150 g (3½–5½ oz) fish per person
for a main course (don't forget, salmon is quite rich), so when buying
the piece of fish with the bone, allow 200 g (7 oz) per person.

NOTE Only take off the skin when you're ready to serve; doing so too
early will result in dry salmon.

Hollandaise Sauce

Serves 4–6

2 egg yolks
1 tbsp water
110 g (4 oz) butter, cut into cubes
squeeze of lemon juice

Put the egg yolks into a saucepan, whisk in 1 tbsp water, then place the saucepan on a very low heat. Gradually whisk in the butter bit by bit; it should emulsify as you whisk it in. The heat should be so low that you should be able to keep your hands on the sides of the saucepan. You can even take it off the heat every now and then, so don't worry.

When all the butter has been added in, taste – it'll need a bit of lemon juice, about 1 tsp. It probably won't need any salt if you have used salted butter. Keep warm in a perspex bowl or jug sitting in a saucepan with about 6 cm (2½ in) of very hot, but not boiling, water. The sauce will keep like this for a couple of hours, just gently heat up the water when it cools down. Leftover hollandaise is excellent in mashed potato.

New Potatoes

Serves 6

1 kg (2¼ lb) new potatoes
sprig of mint
butter
sea salt

Bring a saucepan of water to the boil. Wash the potatoes well and add a sprig of mint into the water with a big pinch of salt. When the water is boiling, tip in the potatoes, cover and boil until they're cooked. If you need to let them sit for a few minutes, drain and leave to sit in the dry saucepan with the lid on with the heat off. They can easily sit like this for half an hour. When ready to serve, put them into a bowl with a few knobs of butter on top and sprinkle with some sea salt.

Pea and Mint Purée

Serves 4

450 g (1 lb) fresh or frozen peas
25 g (1 oz) butter
1 tbsp chopped mint
sea salt and pepper

Cook the peas in boiling water with a pinch of salt, with the lid off, for 3–4 minutes until they are just cooked. Drain and tip into a food processor and whiz up with the butter, mint and some sea salt and pepper to taste. If you're making it ahead of time, make sure that you don't cover it while it's hot, so as to retain the fresh green colour, and don't simmer it for ages, either – just heat it up when you want it.

Mediterranean Shellfish Stew Served with Garlic Crostini

Serves 4

This is a gorgeous light stew, perfect for a summer dinner party. I love it with little Garlic Crostinis, but of course you could serve it with some rice or orzo too.

1 onion, sliced
3 cloves of garlic
1 small red chilli, deseeded and chopped
3 tbsp olive oil
150 ml (5 fl oz) white wine
700 g (1 lb 9 oz) ripe tomatoes, chopped, or 400 g (14 oz) tinned toma-
toes and 4 fresh tomatoes, chopped
12 each of mussels and clams, cleaned and debearded
12 raw prawns, peeled
12 scallops, cut in half
sea salt and pepper
1 tbsp chives
1 tbsp parsley

Cook the onion, garlic and chilli in olive oil in a large saucepan over a medium heat until soft but not coloured. Add the wine and the tomatoes, turn the heat down to low and cook for 25 minutes. Add the mussels, clams (in their shells), prawns and scallops. Place a lid on the pan and cook for about 4 minutes, or until the mussels and clams are wide open and the prawns and scallops are opaque. Discard any shells that haven't opened. Season to taste. Spoon the stew into bowls, sprinkle with the chopped herbs and serve with the Garlic Crostini (page 148).

Asparagus with Chervil or Mint Butter

Serves 4

16 spears fresh green asparagus
50 g (1¾ oz) butter
2 tsp chopped chervil or mint

Snap a tiny bit off the bottom of the asparagus spears, just where it
will snap easily for you, about 3 cm (1 in) from the bottom. Cook in
2 cm (¾ in) of boiling water with a pinch of salt for about 6–8 minutes
or until a knife will pierce the root end easily, but it shouldn't be too
soft. Take it out of the saucepan and drain. Melt the butter in the
saucepan, put the asparagus back in and add the chopped herbs. Serve.

Garlic Crostini

Serves 4-6

100 ml (3½ fl oz) olive oil
5 cloves of garlic, crushed or grated
salt and pepper
½ baguette

Preheat the oven to 220°C/425°F/gas 7. Mix the olive oil with the garlic,
salt and pepper. Cut the baguette into long slices at an angle and brush
with the garlic oil. Place in a single layer on a baking tray and cook in
the oven for about 5 minutes, until pale golden.

Summer Lunch

Pasta with Fresh Tomato, Basil and Ricotta Cheese

Serves 4–6

This has to be made in the summertime with excellent ripe tomatoes.

450 g (1 lb) rigatoni or penne
1 tsp salt
6 large tomatoes
8 large basil leaves
big pinch of sugar
sea salt and pepper
50 ml (2 fl oz) olive oil
125 g (4½ oz) ricotta

Cook the pasta in a large pot of boiling water with 1 tsp of salt until just cooked. While the pasta is cooking, chop the tomatoes into large chunks, about 3 cm (1 in). Tear or slice the basil and add it to the tomatoes with sea salt, pepper, sugar and the olive oil, seasoning to taste. Drain the pasta but keep 50 ml (2 fl oz) of the cooking water and toss with the pasta in a bowl. Season with sea salt, pepper and a pinch of sugar. Throw in the tomatoes, toss gently and put into a large serving bowl or individual bowls and crumble the ricotta over the top.

NOTE In the summertime, when there are so many gorgeous greens around for a salad, I love the simplest salad dressing. Sprinkle a pinch of sea salt over the lettuce with a little freshly ground black pepper. Next, squeeze some lemon juice over the leaves followed by a drizzle of your best olive oil, toss gently and serve. If you want to make this dressing in a jam jar, use 3 parts olive oil to 1 part freshly squeezed lemon juice and a pinch of salt and pepper to taste.

Little Raspberry Cakes

Makes 12 cakes

These are sweet little things. They keep well for a few days and are good with a cup of tea. They also happen to be very quick and easy to make. Feel free to vary the fruit in this recipe – blueberries, quartered strawberries and even blackberries work well. You can halve the recipe if you like, but I never do because I like having these in the house!

175 g (6 oz) butter
175 g (6 oz) icing sugar
50 g (1¾ oz) plain flour
100 g (3½ oz) ground almonds
2 eggs
36–60 raspberries

Preheat the oven to 170°C/325°F/gas 3. Melt the butter and let it cool. With a little of the melted butter, brush the insides of a muffin tin (or 12 ramekins). Sieve the icing sugar and flour together and add the ground almonds. Beat the eggs with a fork and add to the mixture, stirring to combine. Add the cooled melted butter and mix well; it will be quite a soft batter. Pour into the muffin tin and top each one with 3–5 raspberries. Place the cakes in the oven and cook for 14–18 minutes, until just firm in the centre. Wait for a few minutes before trying to take them out of the tins. Dust them with icing sugar.

NOTE If you want these for a picnic, you could always cook the cakes in paper cases in the tin; if doing this, omit 25 g (1 oz) of the butter.

  Summer Lunch

Rhubarb Fool with Strawberries and Jane's Biscuits

Serves 6

The combination of rhubarb and strawberries always tastes like summer to me.

350 g (12 oz) rhubarb, cut into chunks
175 g (6 oz) sugar
2 tbsp water
225 ml (8 fl oz) cream
225 g (9 oz) strawberries, sliced (optional, but I love them in this)

Put the rhubarb into a saucepan with the sugar and water and cook on a gentle heat, stirring regularly for about 20 minutes, until soft. Stir vigorously with a wooden spoon to mash up the rhubarb. Allow to cool completely.

Meanwhile, whip the cream and slice the strawberries. When the rhubarb is cold, gently fold in the whipped cream and the sliced strawberries. Delicious served with Jane's Biscuits (page 152).

NOTE Without the strawberries, any leftover fool will freeze well for a quick rhubarb ice cream.

Jane's Biscuits

Makes about 25 biscuits

These are incredibly simple, gorgeous biscuits. Do make sure the butter
is nice and soft. I always have this recipe in my head in imperial
measurements, as it's just 2, 4, 6 oz.

175 g (6 oz) plain flour
110 g (4 oz) soft butter
60 g (2 oz) caster sugar

Preheat the oven to 180°C/350°F/gas 4. Put the flour into a mixing
bowl, rub in the soft butter, add the sugar and bring the whole mixture
together to form a stiff dough. Do not add any water! Roll the dough
out to about ½ cm (¼ in) thickness and cut into shapes, place carefully
on a baking tray and cook in the oven for 6–10 minutes or until pale
golden. Cool on a wire rack.

NOTE This is such a versatile biscuit recipe. Add ground cinnamon
for cinnamon biscuits, ground ginger, lemon rind, etc. Children love
experimenting with these, making Christmas tree shapes, pigs,
cows, etc.

NOTE Of course, this can be made in a food processor too. Just stop the
machine as soon as it comes together, otherwise it will toughen.

  Summer Lunch

Perfect Pimm's

Makes 10 glasses

1 medium cucumber, peeled and cut into 5 cm (2 in) sticks
4 tbsp chopped fresh mint
150 ml (5 fl oz) freshly squeezed orange juice
150 ml (5 fl oz) freshly squeezed lemon juice
1.8 litres (3 pt) white lemonade
400 ml (14 fl oz) Pimm's
200 ml (7 fl oz) gin
1 twist of orange and 1 twist of lemon for each glass
3–4 strawberries for each glass

Mix all the ingredients in a jug. Serve over ice, making sure each glass
has a twist of orange and lemon, several sticks of cucumber and a few
strawberries. Garnish with a sprig of fresh mint.

Rhubarb Mimosa

Serves 4–10

*200 ml (7 fl oz) poached rhubarb, or use any leftovers from the Rhubarb
Fool (page 151)*
750 ml (1¹⁄₄ pt) bottle of sparkling wine

Liquidise the poached rhubarb (with or without the strawberries from
the Rhubarb Fool recipe) and fill a champagne glass one-quarter full.
Slowly top up with a good chilled sparkling wine.

Winter Lunch

*Like any time of year, make the most of what's
in season now. Go for big hearty stews, traditional roasts,
fruit crumbles and comforting bread and butter puddings,
or simply just a big bowl of warming soup with some
home-made Soda Focaccia.*

Potato and Parsnip Soup with Chorizo

Serves 6–8

50 g (1¾ oz) butter
225 g (8 oz) potatoes, peeled and chopped
225 g (8 oz) parsnips, peeled and chopped
175 g (6 oz) onions, chopped
salt and pepper
850 ml (1½ pt) chicken or vegetable stock
150 ml (5 fl oz) milk, or ½ milk and ½ cream
225 g (8 oz) chorizo or kabanossi sausage, sliced into rounds ¼ cm
(¹⁄₁₀ in) thick
sprig of flat parsley

Melt the butter in a saucepan. Add the potatoes, parsnips and onions,
season with salt and pepper and stir to coat the veggies in butter.
Cover with a butter wrapper (if you have one, otherwise use a disc of
greaseproof paper), put on the lid and sweat over a gentle heat for 10
minutes. Add the stock, bring to the boil and continue cooking until the
vegetables are all soft. Liquidise the soup either in batches in a blender
or with a hand-held blender, add the milk and season to taste.

While the vegetables are cooking, fry the chorizo in a tiny bit of olive
oil in a pan. Take off the heat when it's nice and crisp, reserving the oil.

To serve, put a ladleful of the hot soup into a warmed bowl and top
with about 6 or 7 slices of cooked chorizo. Finish by drizzling a little of
the oil from the pan over the top. Decorate with a few flat parsley
leaves.

NOTE This soup freezes perfectly, and is lovely without the parsnips. If
not using the meat, add some herbs into the soup just before liquidising
it, or drizzle with some Parsley Pesto (page 22) when serving.

White Soda Focaccia with Cheese

Serves 8

Of course, strictly speaking this isn't a focaccia, but I love it anyway. This takes only 10 minutes to make, and it's delicious. I often leave the cheese out and put chunks of raw red onion, whole olives, rosemary leaves and a sprinkle of sea salt on top instead. Experiment and make it your own.

olive oil
450 g (1 lb) plain flour
1 tsp bread soda (bicarbonate of soda, baking soda, they're all the same)
1 level tsp salt
125 g (4½oz) grated cheddar or parmesan
400 ml (14 fl oz) buttermilk

Preheat the oven to 230°C/450°F/gas 8. Brush a swiss roll tin or baking tray generously with olive oil. Sieve the flour and bread soda into a big bowl and add the salt and 50 g (1¾ oz) of the grated cheese. Mix with your hands and make a well in the centre. Pour in most of the buttermilk, and with one hand stiff and your fingers spread out like a claw, start mixing in a full circle once the buttermilk has gone in. Keep mixing like this until you have a soft dough; don't knead it, but rather work it very gently to bring it together.

Transfer to a floured surface and roll it out to about 35 x 20 cm (14 x 8 in) and transfer it to the oiled tray. Press your fingertips into the top to create wells for the olive oil. Brush the top with the oil and sprinkle with the remaining 75 g (2¾ oz) grated cheese. Put it in the oven and cook for 18–25 minutes, depending on how thick it is. Turn the oven down to 200°C/400°C/gas 6 after 10 minutes. When cooked, it should feel firm in the centre and be gorgeously golden brown. Transfer to a wire rack and cool for a couple of minutes, then cut into squares and serve!

Roast Sirloin of Beef Served with Glazed Shallots, Granny's Roast Potatoes and Béarnaise Sauce

Serves 6–8 (you may even have some left over for a steak sandwich)

This has to be one of the best Sunday lunches. This is a big treat, so you won't need to eat for the rest of the day, except for those leftover roast potatoes sneakily dipped into béarnaise – that's the cook's perk! This is for when you have ample time; you won't regret it.

Start with the potatoes, then start the béarnaise. While it's reducing, prepare the shallots, by which time the potatoes will be ready to go into the oven. The beef should be weighed, the cooking time calculated and popped into the oven. Next, put the shallots on to cook; it doesn't matter too much if they're ready a bit early. Then it's time for the béarnaise to be finished – keep it warm while everything finishes cooking.

I honestly think that for this kind of meal, where you have several components, it's worth writing yourself a little order of work (in what order you want to put everything into the oven, etc.) so that you don't suddenly realise when everyone is sitting down that you haven't even started the béarnaise. Also, you can work backwards: if you want the beef to be cooked at 1 pm and it's going to take 1 hour to cook, then put it into the oven at 11:45; this will give you enough time to make the gravy, etc. You can also then relax a bit more because you aren't trying to remember exactly what time the beef needs to be turned down because you have it all written down.

1¹/₂ kg (3 lb 5 oz) sirloin of beef (make sure the beef has been hanging for at least 3 weeks, I prefer 4 weeks; ask your butcher)
olive oil

sea salt and roughly ground pepper
400 ml (14 fl oz) beef or chicken stock

Preheat the oven to 240°C/475°F/gas 9. Lightly score the beef fat and drizzle with a tiny bit of olive oil; season the fat with sea salt and roughly ground black pepper and place, fat side up, in the roasting tray and pop into the hot oven. After 15 minutes reduce the heat to 180°C/350°F/gas 4. Roast until the beef is cooked to your taste (see roasting times below). When cooked, transfer the beef to a serving plate and keep warm while you make the gravy.

To make the gravy, put the tray on the heat on the hob and deglaze by adding about a quarter of the stock. Using a whisk, mix the liquid and all the sweet bits stuck to the tray will dissolve into the juices. Degrease by using a maisgras or pour it into a glass jug, adding a couple of ice cubes to speed up the cooling process, and spoon off the fat as it cools. Pour the degreased liquid into a saucepan, add the rest of the stock, season with salt and pepper and let it boil for about 5 minutes or until you think it's strong enough. Delicious!

NOTE Roasting times for sirloin of beef (weigh the meat first):
If you want RARE meat cook it 8–10 minutes per 450 g (1 lb)
If you want MEDIUM meat cook it 10–12 minutes per 450 g (1 lb)
If you want WELL DONE meat cook it 15–18 minutes per 450 g (1 lb)
Cooking times are approximate as they vary depending on the thickness of the piece of meat.

NOTE Many people who have a tough steak or piece of beef in a restaurant often blame the chef, though often it's actually a case of the beef not being hung for long enough. So if you can, get to know your butcher and he'll give you the best bit!

Glazed Shallots or Baby Onions

Serves 4–6

15–20 shallots or baby onions, peeled
50 g (1¾ oz) butter
1–2 tbsp sugar
150 ml (5 fl oz) red wine or water, or ½ wine, ½ water
salt and pepper

Put the peeled shallots or baby onions into a saucepan with the butter and sugar and toss around for a couple of minutes. Add the wine or water, put on a lid and cook on the hob, or in the hot oven where the beef is cooking, until the onions are cooked. This normally takes about 15–20 minutes. The sauce may be nice and thick by now, but if it isn't, put it on the hob and cook it, uncovered, until it has reduced down to a gorgeous, syrupy glaze. Make sure it doesn't burn.

Winter Lunch

Pasta with Fresh Tomato, Basil and Ricotta Cheese

Roast Chicken with Garlic

Spring Rolls

Spicy Beef Noodle Soup

Lemongrass and Lime Vodkatinis

Birthday Cake

Little Gingerbread Men

Granny's Roast Potatoes

Serves 4–6

My grandmother makes the best roast potatoes, the ones that are crispy and crunchy on the outside and soft on the inside.

8 large potatoes, peeled and cut in half
olive oil or beef drippings
salt

Preheat the oven to 200°C/400°F/gas 6. Drop the potatoes into boiling salted water and cook for 10 minutes. Drain off the water and shake the potatoes in the dry saucepan with the lid on; this makes the edges of the potatoes a bit rough. Heat a few tablespoons of olive oil in a roasting tray and toss the potatoes in it, making sure they are well coated; add more oil if they aren't. Sprinkle with salt and place in the hot oven for 35–55 minutes, spooning the hot oil over them every now and then. Take them out when they're golden brown and crusty.

NOTE If these have to keep warm in the oven for any amount of time, don't cover them. If you do they'll go soggy.

NOTE I sometimes cook these in the same oven as the beef, but not actually in the same tray, and they cook perfectly.

Béarnaise Sauce

Serves 6

One of the great classic sauces to serve with roast beef. Once you follow a few simple points, it's actually not too scary. And is it worth it? Quite definitely yes, I promise you!

4 tbsp white wine
4 tbsp tarragon vinegar or white wine vinegar
2 tsp shallots (1 small shallot or baby onion), finely chopped
pinch of black pepper
2 egg yolks
175 g (6 oz) butter, chopped into 1–2 cm (½–¾ in) pieces
1 tbsp chopped tarragon

Boil the wine, vinegar, chopped shallots and pepper in a saucepan without the lid until they have reduced down to about 1 tbsp of liquid. You really need to watch that this doesn't burn. Let the saucepan cool down until you can place your hand on the bottom of the pan.

When cool, place on a very low heat and whisk in the egg yolks, one by one. The mixture will scramble if the pan is too hot. You can add a drop (1 dessertspoon) of cold water if you think it looks like it's about to scramble. Then add the butter, bit by bit, whisking all the time. Wait for a piece to be emulsified before you add another; you should only have 1 or 2 unmelted pieces in the pan at any one time. The pan shouldn't get too hot; you can pull it on and off the heat while you're making the sauce. The sauce will gradually thicken as all the butter is added. Do not leave the pan or stop whisking until the sauce is made.

When all the butter is added, add the chopped tarragon. You might need more if you're using plain white wine vinegar. Taste for seasoning, though you probably won't need any salt if you're using salted butter.

Keep the sauce warm in a bowl (not stainless steel, it gets too hot) over hot water. If you're careful, you can keep a béarnaise warm for hours.

NOTE To make your own tarragon vinegar, just push 1 or 2 whole sprigs of tarragon into a bottle of white wine vinegar and let sit for a couple of weeks for the flavour to infuse. It will keep for about a year.

NOTE If you have any leftover sauce, you can keep it in the fridge for a couple of days. A bit of it is divine in mashed potatoes or spread onto a toasted baguette for a Steak Sandwich (page 99) instead of the Horseradish Mayonnaise (which it must be said is also really good with the roast sirloin of beef). If you want to heat up leftover béarnaise again (though it's not necessary for a steak sandwich or the mash), boil a couple of tablespoons of cream in a saucepan until thick, let it cool in the pan, then whisk in the béarnaise, bit by bit, on a gentle heat, exactly as you did the butter.

NOTE Béarnaise sauce should be quite thick. If it's too thin, maybe you've been too cautious with the heat. Put it back on a low heat and whisk it gently until it thickens a bit.

Pork Fillet with Mushrooms, White Wine and Sage Leaves

Serves 4–6

Pork fillets (steaks) take no time to prepare, and when sliced take only 10 minutes or so to cook. You can replace the wine with chicken stock.

25 g (1 oz) butter
1 onion, sliced
250 g (9 oz) mushrooms, sliced
2 pork fillets, trimmed of membrane and sliced 1–2 cm (½–¾ in) thick
salt and pepper
1 sprig of sage
2 cloves of garlic, crushed or grated (optional)
150 ml (5 fl oz) white wine
150 ml (5 fl oz) cream
roux (optional; see recipe on page 66)
2 tsp sage, chopped

Melt the butter in a sauté pan, add the onion and sweat over a low heat until soft. Turn up the heat, add the mushrooms and sauté for 2 minutes, then add the sliced pork and sauté until it changes colour. Season with salt and pepper, add a sprig of sage (whole), garlic, if using, the wine and cream. Put the lid on and simmer on the hob for about 10 minutes or until cooked (you could also put it in the oven at 160°C/325°F/gas 3).

Take the pork out of the saucepan when cooked, leaving the sauce in the pan. Put back on the heat and boil, uncovered, until the sauce becomes a little stronger and you're happy with the flavour. Thicken it with roux if you like the sauce slightly thicker. Add the chopped sage and season to taste. This will keep quite well, covered in a warm oven for a little bit. Serve with rice, mashed potato or orzo.

  Winter Lunch

Lamb Shanks with Pot Barley, Red Onions, Celery and Garlic

Serves 4

4 lamb shanks (ask your butcher to saw off the knuckle, if you prefer)
2 tbsp olive oil
2 tbsp pot barley
225 ml (8 fl oz) water
salt and pepper
4 sticks of celery, cut into 6 cm (2½ in) chunks
2 large red onions, peeled and cut in quarters down through the root
8 cloves of garlic, more if you like, peeled

Preheat the oven to 140°C/275°F/gas 1. Trim the shanks of excess fat. Put a casserole or oven-proof saucepan on a medium heat on the hob and add the olive oil. Sauté the shanks until browned all over. Add the pot barley, pour in the water, sprinkle in some salt and pepper, put the lid on and place in the oven for 1 hour 15 minutes.

Meanwhile, prepare the vegetables. After 1 hour 15 minutes add the celery, onions and garlic and continue to cook for another 30–45 minutes, or until the vegetables are soft and the lamb is tender and almost falling off the bone. Remove from the oven and strain off the juices. Skim the fat off the top of the juices and add back into the lamb. This is great with Mustard Mash (page 52) or Pea and Spring Onion Champ (page 129).

Roast Chicken with Garlic

Serves 4–6

When garlic is roasted it loses its strong edge and develops a delicious, sweet flavour. It's wonderful with the chicken.

4 heads of garlic – no, this isn't a misprint!
1 good-quality chicken
salt and pepper
25 g (1 oz) soft butter
sea salt for the top
whole black peppercorns or freshly ground black pepper
juice of 1 lemon
350 ml (12 fl oz) chicken stock, for the gravy

Preheat the oven to 190°C/375°F/gas 5. Slice the top and bottom off the heads of garlic, separate the cloves and peel them. Place the chicken in the roasting tray. Put about 8 cloves of peeled garlic in the cavity of the chicken, along with a pinch of salt and pepper. Smear the soft butter over the skin. Sprinkle with some flakes of sea salt and some freshly ground black pepper (the pepper should be quite rough – bash it in a pestle and mortar or in a plastic bag with a rolling pin) and lightly push it into the butter. Pour over the juice of 1 lemon and pop into the preheated oven for 30 minutes, then add the remaining garlic cloves around the chicken, basting them and the bird with the juices. Roast for a further 45–60 minutes, until cooked. The legs should feel quite loose in the bird, and when a skewer is stuck into the thigh, with a spoon placed underneath to catch the juices, the juices should run clear.

Transfer the chicken and the garlic cloves to a serving plate and leave to rest, in a warm oven if possible, while you make the gravy. Place the roasting tray on the hob on a medium heat, add half of the stock and bring to the boil, whisking to deglaze the sweet juicy bits which have

stuck to the tray. When it comes to the boil, pour it into a maisgras or a small bowl or glass jug. If using the bowl/jug, add 1 or 2 ice cubes. This will draw the fat to the top; then you can spoon the fat off and discard. If using a maisgras, degrease the juices in the usual way. Pour the degreased juices into a small saucepan, add the remainder of the stock, bring to the boil and season to taste. If it's a little watery, boil it for another couple of minutes. Take the chicken out of the oven, carve and serve with the gravy, Granny's Roast Potatoes (page 161) or mash or Gratin of Potatoes and Leeks (page 116).

NOTE You could leave out the garlic and pop a lemon into the cavity.

NOTE In the wintertime, when there isn't very much exciting green salad stuff available, don't forget about cabbage, which is in season this time of year. Some finely shredded red cabbage makes for a winter salad with lovely flavour and crunch.

Orzo

Serves 4–6

Orzo is pasta shaped like a large grain of rice. It's great with the pork on page 164, as it soaks up all the delicious sauce. It's also good with lots of chopped herbs through it and is a good base for a salad.

225 g (8 oz) orzo
butter or olive oil

Bring a saucepan of water to the boil and add a good pinch of salt. Drop in the orzo, stir and boil until it's cooked, about 8–10 minutes. Drain all the cooking liquid except for a couple of tablespoons and toss with a drizzle of olive oil or a small knob of butter. Put it into a bowl and cover with a plate or tin foil and keep warm until serving.

Chocolate Meringues with Chocolate Cream

Makes 16–20 meringues

for the chocolate meringues:
3 egg whites
150 g (5½ oz) caster sugar
2 tsp cocoa, sieved
50 g (1¾ oz) good dark chocolate, grated or chopped finely (can whiz in a food processor)

for the chocolate cream:
100 g (3½ oz) chocolate
50 ml (2 fl oz) cream

Preheat the oven to 140°C/275°F/gas 1 and line 2 baking trays with greaseproof paper. In a perfectly dry, clean bowl, whisk the egg whites until almost stiff. Gradually add the sugar, whisking all the time. Stop whisking when it's very thick and will hold stiff peaks. In a separate bowl, stir together the cocoa and chocolate and gently fold into the meringue. Spoon tablespoonfuls of the mixture onto the prepared trays and quickly put into the oven before it loses any volume. Cook for 40 minutes or until they lift easily off the paper.

To make the chocolate cream, gently melt the chocolate with the cream, stir to mix, pour into a bowl and let it cool; it will thicken as it cools. This can be done in advance, but don't put the chocolate cream into the fridge, as it won't be easy to spread on the meringues if you do.

When the meringues and chocolate cream are cool, sandwich the meringues with a tablespoonful of the chocolate cream. These sit perfectly like this for a couple of hours. If you like, serve with some softly whipped cream.

  Winter Lunch

NOTE Ideally, meringues shouldn't be taken out of the hot oven and placed somewhere cold, as the sudden change in temperature causes them to crack. So if you can, when they're cooked just turn off the oven and let them cool down slowly.

NOTE 1 egg white equals 25 g (1 oz) or 25 ml (1 fl oz), so if you can't remember how many are in that bowl in the fridge, you can measure them. Egg whites keep very well in the fridge for a couple of weeks and they also freeze well in an airtight container or tied up in a plastic bag. Just thaw out overnight in the fridge.

Marmalade Bread and Butter Pudding

Serves 6–8

This is a variation on basic bread and butter pudding. If you like, leave out the marmalade and serve plain, or add chopped rhubarb, chopped chocolate, grated lemon or orange zest, raisins, sultanas, cinnamon, nutmeg, etc. This is a great way to use up stale bread, and in fact is better if the bread is stale.

12 slices of good-quality white bread, crusts removed
50 g (1¾ oz) soft butter
3 tbsp marmalade
450 ml (16 oz) cream
225 ml (8 fl oz) milk
4 eggs
150 g (5½ oz) caster sugar
2 tbsp granulated sugar

Preheat the oven to 180°C/350°F/gas 4. Butter the bread and spread marmalade on each slice. Arrange the bread in the gratin dish or in individual cups or bowls (cut the slices if you need to). I like to have overlapping triangles of bread on the top layer.

Place the cream and milk in a saucepan and bring to just under the boil. While it's heating up, in a separate bowl whisk the eggs and sugars, then pour the hot milk and cream in with the eggs and whisk to combine. Pour this custard over the bread and leave to soak for 10 minutes. Place in a bain marie (water bath) and cook in the preheated oven for 1 hour. The top should be golden and the centre should be just set. Serve with softly whipped cream.

NOTE If you want to make this a day ahead of time, don't heat up the milk and cream, just pour it cold over the bread.

Winter Lunch

Mulled Cider

Serves 3–4

I'm not suggesting you drink this with a meal; this is best when you've just returned from a big walk (or a little one!) outside. Great at Christmastime as a change to hot port and mulled wine; it's just as good if made with non-alcoholic, good-quality apple juice too.

500 ml (18 fl oz) medium-dry cider or good-quality apple juice
100 ml (3½ fl oz) water
50 g (1¾ oz) Demerara sugar
6 cm (2 in) piece of cinnamon stick, broken in half
2 strips of orange rind, removed with a peeler
2 whole cloves

Place everything in a saucepan and heat up, stirring to dissolve the sugar. Serve.

Blackberry and Apple Crumble

Serves 6

3–4 large cooking apples, peeled, cored and cut into big chunks
1 tbsp water
2–3 tbsp sugar
225 g (8 oz) blackberries – frozen is okay

for the crumble:
175 g (6 oz) plain white flour
75 g (2¾ oz) butter
75 g (2¾ oz) Demerara sugar

Preheat the oven to 180°C/350°F/gas 4. Put the apple chunks, water and sugar into a saucepan over a low heat and cook until the apples are soft and pulpy, about 10 minutes. While it's cooking, stir it every minute or so to prevent it sticking to the bottom of the saucepan. Taste and add more sugar if it needs it. Transfer the apple pulp into individual bowls or 1 big pie dish and allow to cool slightly. Put the blackberries on top of the apple now.

To make the crumble, rub the butter into the flour until the mixture resembles coarse breadcrumbs (if you rub it in too much, the crumble won't be crunchy). Add the sugar. Sprinkle this crumble mixture over the slightly cooled apple and bake for 15 minutes for small crumbles or 30–45 minutes for large crumbles, or until the crumble is cooked and golden. Serve warm with whipped cream or vanilla ice cream.

NOTE The apple pulp is basically the same as apple sauce, as you would serve with roast pork, so this is a great way of using up any leftover apple sauce.

NOTE If you prefer to leave out the blackberries, you could add ½ tsp

ground cinnamon or a few cloves to the apple. Crumbles can be made with practically any fruit.

NOTE I sometimes use different sugars in the crumble, such as dark brown, caster, etc. I also occasionally put some oats into the crumble or nuts, like chopped pecans, walnuts, almonds, etc.

NOTE If you want to use less sugar, you can cook eating apples instead of the cooking variety. When cooked, eating apples have a slightly less fluffy texture, but it will still be good; just cut out most of the sugar when cooking the apples.

NOTE For a summertime rhubarb and strawberry crumble, just cook the rhubarb as you would for the Rhubarb Fool with Strawberries (page 151), but don't reduce it until it's too thick, let it be a bit more juicy. Add the sliced strawberries (but not the cream), cover with the crumble and bake as above.

Noodles

*Rice noodles, soba noodles, udon noodles, egg noodles...
there's a whole world of noodles out there. A big bowl of
noodles is a meal in a dish and so delicious to eat.
I always think they feel good for the soul.*

Thai Coconut Soup with Pak Choi and Rice Noodles

Serves 4–6

So quick, easy and good for the soul. Can be a meal in itself.

100 g (3½ oz) medium flat rice noodles, about ½ cm (¼ in) wide
400 ml (14 fl oz) tin of coconut milk
400 ml (14 fl oz) chicken or vegetable stock or water
2 tbsp grated ginger
1 chilli, chopped or 1 pinch of dried chilli flakes
2 cloves of garlic, crushed
2 tbsp nam pla (Thai fish sauce)
450 g (1 lb) pak choi, sliced
2 tbsp chopped coriander

Soak the rice noodles in boiling water for 10 minutes or until soft and drain. Place the coconut milk, stock, ginger, chilli, garlic and fish sauce into a saucepan, bring up to the boil and cook for 5 minutes. Add the pak choi and continue cooking for another 5 minutes, until pak choi is just soft. Add the chopped coriander. Using tongs, divide the noodles (it doesn't matter if they've cooled down by now) into deep serving bowls and pour a ladleful of the hot soup over them. Serve.

NOTE I have often made this at home when I haven't had any fresh coriander or pak choi and it's still delicious. You could even use parsley. For meat eaters, thinly sliced cooked chicken breast in place of the pak choi is great.

NOTE You can cut the noodles to make them easier to eat, but in many parts of Asia it's very bad luck to cut noodles, it's like cutting all your hopes and dreams! Besides, I prefer slurping and sucking up the noodles.

Japanese Chicken and Udon Noodle Soup

Serves 6

Udon noodles are made from a flour and water dough and can be round, square or flat. In most recipes you can replace udon noodles with soba noodles, Chinese noodles or, as a last resort, spaghetti.

225 g (8 oz) finely shredded raw chicken breast
2 tbsp rice wine or sake
2 cm (³/₄ in) piece of ginger, slightly bashed with a rolling pin but still in one piece
225 g (8 oz) udon noodles or soba noodles
1 litre (1³/₄ pt) of light chicken stock or instant dashi, to make 1 litre (1³/₄ pt)
3 tbsp mirin (sweetened rice wine); if you can't get this, you can use white wine
5 tbsp Japanese soy sauce
225 g (8 oz) sugar snaps or mange tout, topped, tailed, stringy bits removed and cut in half
4 tbsp spring onions, sliced at an angle

Place the shredded chicken into a bowl with the rice wine and ginger and toss lightly to coat. Bring a large saucepan of water to the boil, drop in the noodles and stir to prevent them from sticking. Bring back to the boil and cook for 3–5 minutes, until just tender. Drain in a colander and rinse under warm water, still in the colander. Divide the noodles between the serving bowls. Pour the stock (or dashi), the mirin and the soy sauce into a saucepan and bring to the boil. Add the chicken and cook for just 2 minutes, skimming any impurities from the surface. Add the sugar snaps and continue to cook for 1 more minute or until the chicken and sugar snaps are just cooked. Taste for seasoning and add soy sauce as needed. Ladle the broth with some chicken and sugar snaps over the udon noodles in the bowls and sprinkle with some sliced spring onions to serve.

NOTE Dashi, a basic Japanese soup stock, is made from kelp (konbu) and dried bonito fish flake. Available at some health food shops and Asian stores.

Noodle Salad with Chicken and Mint

Serves 6

This is a light salad with lots of fresh mint. You feel great after eating something like this.

375 g (13 oz) dried thin rice noodles (vermicelli) or glass noodles (made from mung beans)
3–4 chicken breasts, cooked on a grill pan/frying pan and shredded
1 handful of mint leaves, shredded
75 g (2¾ oz) grated carrots or bean sprouts
3 tbsp toasted sesame seeds

for the dressing:
1 chilli, deseeded and chopped
2 tbsp sugar
3 tbsp lime juice
3 tbsp nam pla (Thai fish sauce)
3 tbsp toasted cashew nuts, roughly chopped

Place the noodles into a bowl, cover with boiling water and allow to sit for 3–5 minutes, then drain. Toss the chicken with the mint, carrots, sesame seeds, and noodles. In a separate bowl, mix all the ingredients for the dressing together and pour over the salad. Sprinkle with the toasted cashew nuts.

Vietnamese Prawns with Coriander and Rice Noodles

Serves 6

I absolutely adore the sweet and sour flavours in this dressing. The sugar and the saltiness of the fish sauce are perfectly offset by the heat of the chilli.

700 g (1 lb 9 oz) tiger prawns, peeled, scored down the back, deveined, rinsed and patted dry
2 tsp finely grated ginger
2 tsp nam pla (Thai fish sauce)
110 g (4 oz) thin rice noodles, softened in boiling water for 5 minutes, drained and rinsed
2 tbsp sunflower oil
110 g (4 oz) mange tout, cut in half, or bean sprouts, rinsed and drained
110 g (4 oz) spring onions, sliced
75 g (2¾ oz) peanuts, toasted under the grill until golden (rub off skins, then blow them away outside) and chopped
2 tbsp chopped coriander

for the dressing (makes 250 ml/9 fl oz):
100 ml (3½ fl oz) fish sauce
100 ml (3½ fl oz) Japanese rice vinegar
50 g (1¾ oz) sugar or more to taste
2 small chillies, deseeded and finely sliced
4 cloves of garlic, crushed

To make the dressing, mix all the ingredients together and add more sugar or soy sauce if it needs it.

In a bowl, toss together the prawns with the ginger and fish sauce.

Arrange the noodles on 6 serving plates or 1 large plate. Heat a wok, add 1 tbsp of the oil and cook the prawns until they're just cooked, about 2–3 minutes. Add the mange tout and spring onions and cook for 1 more minute. Transfer to the plate on top of the noodles. Sprinkle over the toasted peanuts, coriander and dressing. Serve either hot or cold.

Ginger Pork with Noodles

Serves 4

Because of the Chinese hoisin sauce, this is slightly sweet. It's also good without the basil. This is a great quick meal in a bowl.

200 g (7 oz) thick rice noodles
1 tbsp peanut, sunflower or groundnut oil
2 tbsp grated ginger
500 g (1 lb 2 oz) minced pork
50 ml (2 fl oz) hoisin sauce
100 ml (3½ fl oz) chicken stock
2 tbsp chopped coriander
1 tbsp shredded basil

Put the rice noodles in boiling water and cook for about 8 minutes or until tender. Drain. While the noodles are cooking, heat the oil in a frying pan or wok, add the ginger and pork and cook for about 5 minutes. Add the hoisin sauce and chicken stock and cook for 2 more minutes. Toss in the coriander, basil and noodles, season to taste and serve straight away.

Spring Rolls

Makes about 20 medium or 40 tiny spring rolls

These are great for a party, as they can be made up in advance, then cooked closer to the time. Have everything ready in bowls for this, all chopped and grated.

3 tbsp sesame oil
4 cloves of garlic, finely chopped
2 cm (¾ in) piece of ginger, finely chopped
20 peeled raw tiger prawns, cut in half
150 g (5½ oz) mushrooms, sliced
1–2 tbsp soy sauce
200 g (7 oz) carrots, grated
200 g (7 oz) green cabbage, finely sliced and core removed
50 g (1¾ oz) spring onions, chopped
100 g (3½ oz) peanuts, toasted under the grill (rub off skins, then blow them away outside), then chopped
50 g (1¾ oz) glass noodles (cellophane, mung bean) or rice vermicelli or thin egg noodles, soaked in boiling water for 3-5 minutes until soft, then drained, rinsed and cut up a bit
20 spring roll wrappers (these are available from supermarkets and Asian food stores)

Heat a wok or frying pan until hot. Add 2 tbsp of the sesame oil and the garlic and ginger. Stir and fry for about 45 seconds, until it's just starting to turn pale golden. Add the prawns immediately and cook for a few minutes, until opaque and just cooked. Take them out of the pan and set aside in a large bowl. Add more oil if you need it and fry the mushrooms until cooked. Add the soy sauce, then add the mushrooms to the prawns. Fry the carrots and cabbage just until the vegetables begin to wilt. Take out and add to the prawns and mushrooms, then throw in the spring onions, peanuts and the cut noodles and taste for soy sauce and salt.

To assemble your spring rolls, separate the spring roll wrappers and place them under a damp cloth to prevent them from drying out. Lay a spring roll wrapper in front of you, in the shape of a diamond. Place a generous tablespoonful of the mixture a quarter of the way up the wrapper. Then roll the edge closest to you up onto the mixture and roll it away from you twice. Fold in the sides, and continue rolling it away from you until it resembles a cylinder. Brush the very tip of the wrapper at the furthest point away from you with a mixture of flour and water (1 tsp flour, stirred with 1 tbsp water) to keep it secure. Repeat the process with the rest of the mixture, and deep fry or shallow fry in a few tablespoons of oil (sunflower or groundnut). These will keep warm if left uncovered in a warm oven. To make tiny ones, cut the wrappers in half. Lay it out as a rectangle in front of you, and on the bottom quarter, place 1 tsp of the mixture. Roll it away from you twice then fold in the sides, and continue rolling away from you, not forgetting to brush the last bit with the water and flour mix to seal.

Dip these spring rolls in sweet chilli sauce or Thai Dipping Sauce (page 60).

NOTE This is also really good without rolling the mixture in spring roll wrappers. Served hot as a stir fry (just toss everything in the hot pan) it would serve 6.

NOTE I also love this made with beef instead of the prawns. Use 400 g (14 oz) of flank or rump of beef, very thinly sliced, and cook as for the prawns.

NOTE Try and buy a 50 g (1¾ oz) packet of glass noodles as they are very difficult to separate before cooking. I would also recommend using rice vermicelli (thin rice noodles) or thin egg noodles.

Spicy Beef Noodle Soup

Serves 4

There is serious eating and drinking in this soup. For a great cure for a cold increase the red curry paste, which consists of red chillies, garlic, lemongrass and galangal among other ingredients. I love having red curry paste in the fridge. I must admit I buy mine rather than making it, as this soup is normally made when I don't want to spend ages in the kitchen. The brand I use is Mae Ploy; it's great and has no added preservatives or nasty colourants. This soup also happens to be a good hangover cure!

200 g (7 oz) fine egg noodles
50 ml (2 fl oz) sunflower oil
1 x 400 ml (14 fl oz) tin of coconut milk (the brand I prefer is Chaokoh)
150 ml (5 fl oz) water
1½–2 tsp red curry paste
300 g (10½ oz) stewing beef, with the fat removed and sliced into very thin strips
1 tsp brown sugar
¾–1 tbsp nam pla (Thai fish sauce)
75 g (2¾ oz) mange tout or sugar snaps, cooked for 2 minutes in boiling water, then drained in cold water
2 tbsp roughly chopped coriander leaves (you can use the fine stalks too) or Thai basil

Bring a saucepan of water to a boil. Add the noodles, stir and bring back to the boil, then place the lid on the saucepan and remove from the heat. Leave to sit for 3 minutes or until cooked. Drain and rinse under cold water. Take out a quarter of the drained noodles and place on kitchen paper to dry completely. Divide the remaining noodles between 4 deep bowls. Next, fry the noodles on the kitchen paper in the sunflower oil for 1 minute or until pale golden brown. Drain on

kitchen paper again. Put the coconut milk, water and red curry paste into a saucepan and bring to a boil. Add the slices of beef and continue to simmer for 4 or 5 minutes or until the beef is cooked. Add the brown sugar, fish sauce and mange tout and taste. You probably will not need any salt, as the fish sauce is quite salty itself. Ladle into the deep bowls, then crumble the fried noodles on top and add a scattering of coriander leaves.

NOTE Feel free to vary this, replacing the beef for chicken, or leave meat out altogether if you like. If you don't want to fry the noodles, don't; I like the contrast of textures though.

Sesame and Peanut Noodles

Serves 4–6

This is a really fast noodle dish that uses peanut butter as the base
for the sauce. It is served at room temperature. You can leave out the
chicken if you like, and you can substitute the cucumber and red
pepper with carrot and beansprouts.

for the sesame peanut sauce (makes 150 ml/5 fl oz):
2 cloves of garlic, crushed or finely grated
2 tsp ginger, finely grated
2 generous tbsp crunchy peanut butter
2 tbsp toasted sesame oil
2 tbsp soy sauce
*2 tbsp rice wine (sake) (I have used white wine in an emergency, and it's
fine)*
2 tbsp water
2 tsp brown sugar
3 tbsp toasted sesame seeds + 1 tbsp for sprinkling over the top

250 g (9 oz) fine egg noodles
1 tbsp toasted sesame oil
1/2 large cucumber (about 200 g/7 oz)) cut into matchsticks
1 red pepper, cut in quarters, then sliced across into very thin strips
*2 chicken breasts, cooked (pan-fried, grilled, roasted) then cut into very
thin strips*
3 spring onions, sliced thinly across at an angle

First make the peanut sesame sauce. Mix the garlic, ginger and peanut
butter, then add the rest of the ingredients for the sauce, making sure
the peanut butter is evenly mixed and not lumpy. Place the noodles
into a saucepan of boiling water, bring the water back to the boil and
stir the noodles. Place a lid on the saucepan, turn off the heat and

leave to sit in the saucepan for 3 minutes, by which time they should be cooked. Drain the noodles, rinse with cold water, drain again, then toss with 1 tbsp toasted sesame oil. Place the noodles in a large bowl with the cucumber, red pepper and chicken, and pour in most of the sauce. Toss together and add more sauce if desired. Transfer to a serving bowl (if it's not already in it) and sprinkle the sliced spring onion and 1 tbsp sesame seeds over the top.

NOTE This sesame peanut sauce keeps well in the fridge for about a week, and it's great to dip chicken into or have with barbecued meats.

NOTE When buying toasted sesame oil look at the label; it should be pure toasted sesame oil, not blended with other oils, otherwise it will be too weak in flavour.

Coconut Rice Pudding with Orange and Cardamom

Serves 4

In Asia a sweet rice pudding is often served after eating rice or noodles for a main course. This is great served either on its own or with the Spiced Nectarines.

150 g (5½ oz) short grain pudding rice
400 ml (14 fl oz) tin of coconut milk
225 ml (8 fl oz) milk
100 g (3½ oz) caster sugar
finely grated zest of 1 orange
1 tsp of freshly ground cardamom seeds, extracted from green cardamom pods

Preheat the oven to 150°C/300°F/gas 2. Put all the ingredients in a saucepan (it will 'expand' as the rice cooks, so don't choose a saucepan too small) and bring up to the boil. Stir to dissolve the sugar, place a lid on top and transfer to the preheated oven. Cook for 45 minutes or until the rice is completely cooked and all the liquid has been absorbed. You can cook this on the hob, but it must be on a very low heat so it will not burn on the bottom. Serve warm. If you want to reheat this just add a drop of water and stir until it is warm again.

Spiced Nectarines

Serves 4

These delicious nectarines are wonderful after a spicy meal, served with or without the Coconut Rice Pudding. Without the rice pudding I would serve them with a blob of crème fraîche or Greek yoghurt. Of course you can also use peaches.

100 g (3½ oz) caster sugar
100 ml (3½ fl oz) water
1 tbsp white wine vinegar
20 green cardamom pods, slightly bashed but seeds not taken out
6 cm (2 in) cinnamon stick, slightly bashed
4 nectarines

Put the sugar, water, vinegar, cardamom pods and cinnamon into a saucepan and bring to the boil, stirring to dissolve the sugar. Take out the spoon and boil for 2 minutes while you prepare the nectarines. Cut them in half, remove the stone and place in the saucepan of syrup. Cook on the hob with the lid on for 15 minutes or until the nectarines are nice and soft. Serve warm or cold. These keep very well for 4 or 5 days in the fridge.

NOTE For plain poached nectarines, cook these without the vinegar and spices to serve with yoghurt for breakfast or pudding with ice cream.

Lemongrass and Lime Vodkatinis

Serves 2

These are great to get the palate kick-started for a spicy meal ahead –
actually, they are good anytime!

25 g (1 oz) caster sugar
*1 stalk lemongrass, chopped (first remove the tough top part of the stalk
and outer leaves)*
2 tsp ginger, grated
8 mint leaves, chopped
50 ml (2 fl oz) boiling water
8 cubes of ice
100 ml (3½ fl oz) vodka
juice of 1 lime

Put the sugar, lemongrass, ginger and mint into a bowl and pour in the
boiling water (must be boiling), stir to combine and let infuse for 10
minutes or until cool. Strain, then add the vodka and lime juice, shake
with ice (or stir in a jug with ice), remove the ice then serve in a frozen
glass with a mint leaf floating on top.

NOTE If you don't have lemongrass, use finely grated rind of the lime
instead.

NOTE For a non-boozy version, use some sparkling water instead of the
vodka.

NOTE These are good served with crushed ice too.

Children's
Birthday Party

Something that parents both look forward to and dread at the same time, a children's birthday party need not be a huge amount of work – I mean the cooking for it, anyway! In my experience of parties, the children will not actually notice or appreciate the fact that you have been cooking for 48 hours for the occasion, so keep it simple and just serve a few really good things.

Sandwiches Cut into Shapes

I definitely find that for my two-year-old and four-year-old, if something is cut into a funny shape, they will eat it much more enthusiastically. Not that I cut everything up, just some things, like toast and sandwiches for a birthday party. Use any biscuit cutters you like: stars, pigs, fish, trains, boys, girls, whatever. Basically, when you've made your sandwich, press it down with your hands or a rolling pin to squash it a little bit, then cut a couple of shapes out. You'll find that there isn't too much waste if you're careful. You can even whiz up the remaining bread to make breadcrumbs.

Toad in the Hole

Serves 12–18

My children love this name! This is the same batter used for Yorkshire puddings; just omit the sausages.

110 g (4 oz) plain flour
pinch of salt
2 eggs
300 ml (10 fl oz) milk
10 g (1/2 oz) butter, melted and cooled
olive or sunflower oil
24 cocktail sausages, cooked

You will also need a bun tray or a muffin tin.

Preheat the oven to 230°C/350°F/gas 8. Sieve the flour and salt into a bowl, make a well in the centre and add the eggs. Whisk continuously, drawing the flour in from the sides of the bowl. Add the milk in gradually while whisking. Add the cooled melted butter. Place the tin into the hot oven on its own for a couple of minutes to heat up, then put a generous

Children's Birthday Party

tsp of oil into each muffin cup and 2 cooked sausages. Fill each cup three-quarters full with the batter and put into the hot oven for 15–20 minutes or until golden brown.

NOTE You can make this batter ahead of time. In fact, it makes these even lighter if you do.

NOTE From this batter you could also make American-style popovers, often served at brunch. Omit the sausages, add 2 tbsp caster sugar to the flour and cook as above. When they're cooked and cool, place a teaspoonful of marmalade or raspberry jam into the dip in the centre. Dust with icing sugar, if you like.

White or Milk Chocolate Chewy Rice Krispie Buns

Makes 24 mini buns

These slightly chewy Rice Krispie buns are so good. The white chocolate ones are very handy if you don't want dark chocolate mess all over the children's clothes!

75 g (2¾ oz) white chocolate or milk chocolate
2 tbsp golden syrup
25 g (1 oz) Rice Krispies

Melt the chocolate with the golden syrup in a large glass bowl sitting over a saucepan of simmering water. Add the Rice Krispies and gently fold in. Spoon into mini bun cases. Put into the fridge for half an hour to set. These are best eaten within 24 hours.

NOTE You can also add some raisins into this mixture.

Mini Buns with Coloured Icing

Makes 24 mini buns or 12 normal buns

I almost always make mini buns for a birthday because, in my experience, the children only want a little taste of everything and I'm sick of finding half-eaten buns around the house days later! I adore this coloured sugar on top of buns, it reminds me of something out of a fairytale and looks quite chic and girly too.

110 g (4 oz) butter
110 g (4 oz) sugar
2 eggs, whisked
1/4 tsp vanilla essence
140 g (5 oz) plain flour mixed with 1/4 tsp baking powder

for the icing:
100 g (3½ oz) icing sugar
boiling water
food colouring – red (which also makes pink icing), blue, yellow, green, whatever you like!

for the decorations:
Smarties
jelly tots
hundreds and thousands, etc.
chocolate buttons
coloured sugar

for the coloured sugar:
100 g (3½ oz) icing sugar
food colouring

Preheat the oven to 190°C/375°F/gas 5. Cream the butter, add the sugar and beat until light. Gradually add the beaten eggs, then the vanilla.

Fold in the flour and baking powder and bring together (or put all the ingredients into a food processor and whiz up until it comes together). Put into mini bun cases sitting in mini bun trays and cook for 7–10 minutes. Cool on a wire rack before you ice them.

To make the icing, sieve the icing sugar into a bowl and add about 2 tsp of boiling water and a single drop (or more if you want bright, gaudy icing!) of your chosen food colouring. Beat with a wooden spoon and add another drop of water if it's too stiff to spread over the top of a bun, and add more food colouring if you want a deeper colour. If you've made it too wet, just add more icing sugar. This will make enough to ice about 20–30 mini buns. I like to make a few different colours.

Then, when the icing is made, take a small palette knife or a table knife and dip it into a cup of boiling water. This will make it easier to spread the icing and it will give it a nice glossy shine. If you want to decorate the muffins, put it on now, before the icing sets.

To make coloured sugar, put 100 g (3½ oz) of icing sugar and 1 or 2 drops of your chosen colouring into a sieve and sieve into a bowl, then sieve it all again. Keep doing this (maybe another 2 times) until the food colouring has tinted the sugar. Spread a very thin layer of icing on each muffin (use only about ¼ of the icing recipe) and dip the top of the bun into the coloured sugar. Cute!

NOTE You could add raisins or chocolate chips to the flour.

Little Gingerbread Men

Makes about 20

110 g (4 oz) butter
55 g (2 oz) caster sugar
55 g (2 oz) brown sugar
½ egg, beaten
2 tbsp treacle
300 g (10½ oz) plain flour
2 tsp ground ginger
¾ tsp bread soda
½ tsp ground cinnamon
¼ tsp ground nutmeg
pinch of salt

for the icing (optional):
75 g (2¾ oz) icing sugar
boiling water

You will also need boy and girl biscuit cutters for these.

Preheat the oven to 170°C/325°F/gas 3. Line 2 baking trays with parchment paper. Cream the butter, add the sugars and beat until light and fluffy. Add the egg and treacle and blend well. Sieve the remaining dry ingredients, then stir into the butter mixture. Knead the mixture for a second or two until it comes together. Roll the dough out a little, chill for 10 minutes, then continue to roll to about ½ cm (¼ in) thick (chilling makes rolling easier). Cut out the girl and boy shapes and transfer onto the trays. Cook for 12–15 minutes, until firm at the edges. Place on a wire rack to cool.

To make the icing, sieve the icing sugar into a bowl and add about 2 tsp of boiling water. Beat with a wooden spoon and add another drop of water if it's to stiff to spread. If you've made it too wet, just add more sugar.

  Children's Birthday Party

Toffee Popcorn and Plain Popcorn

Makes about 1½ litres (2¾ pt)

This recipe makes enough for plain popcorn and toffee popcorn, as I like having both, but if you want just one kind, then use half the popcorn.

2 tbsp sunflower oil
75 g (2¾ oz) popcorn kernels

for toffee popcorn:
40 g (1½ oz) butter
40 g (1½ oz) brown sugar
2 tbsp golden syrup
pinch salt
25 g (1 oz) butter

Heat the oil in a big saucepan. Add the popcorn kernels and swirl the pan to coat the popcorn in oil. Put the lid on, turn the heat down to low and listen for the popping! As soon as the popping almost stops, take it off the heat to avoid burning the bottom.

To make toffee popcorn, melt the butter, add the brown sugar and golden syrup and stir over a high heat for 1–2 minutes. When the popcorn has all popped, tip half of it out of the saucepan and toss with 25 g (1 oz) butter and a pinch of salt. Pour the toffee over the remaining popcorn, put the lid on the pan and shake to mix the toffee sauce. Pour out into bowls and allow to cool a little.

Birthday Cake

Serves 8

This cake doesn't have any butter, so even with lots of lovely whipped cream it still seems light.

3 eggs, separated
225 g (8 oz) sugar
90 ml (3 fl oz) water
140 g (5 oz) flour, sieved
1 tsp baking powder

for the filling:
250 ml (9 fl oz) whipped cream
85 g (3¼ oz) fresh fruit, like sliced strawberries or whole raspberries
2 tsp icing sugar

Preheat the oven to 180°C/350°F/gas 4. Beat the egg yolks and sugar for 2 minutes. Blend in the water and whisk until firm and creamy, about 10 minutes. Fold in the flour and baking powder. In a separate clean, dry bowl, beat the egg whites until they hold a stiff peak. Fold them into the flour mixture very gently. Bake in 2 greased and floured 20 cm (8 in) sandwich tins for about 20 minutes. Cool on a wire rack and fill with whipped cream and fresh fruit. Sift the icing sugar on top before serving.

NOTE I have made this before with just one 20 cm (8 in) springform tin, in which case cook it for 35 minutes, or until the centre feels firm to the touch. I also put a sheet of tin foil on top of the cake and turn the oven down to 170°C/325°F/gas 3 after 20 minutes.

  Children's Birthday Party

Peanut Butter Cookies

Makes about 30 biscuits

These are light, crisp and ever so slightly chewy. I could eat these all day, and at birthday parties, I do!

200 g (7 oz) crunchy peanut butter
150 g (5½ oz) caster sugar
1 egg
1 tsp bread soda, sieved (baking soda, bicarbonate of soda, it's all the same)

Preheat the oven to 180°C/350°F/gas 4. Mix the peanut butter and sugar together. In a separate bowl, whisk the egg and add the sieved bread soda, then add to the peanut butter and sugar and mix with a wooden spoon until combined. Roll into balls (whatever size you like, they will spread a little bit) and place a few centimetres away from each other on 2 baking trays (no need to line or grease them). Wet a fork and slightly flatten them. Bake for 10–15 minutes or until pale golden. Allow to cool for a minute before transferring them to a wire rack. These keep very well and, of course, freeze.

Laura O'Mahony's Marshmallow Krispies

Makes 15 pieces

I have an incredibly sweet tooth, so I adore these!

100 g (3½ oz) wrapped toffees or a slab of toffee from your newsagent
100 g (3½ oz) butter
100 g (3½ oz) marshmallows
100 g (3½ oz) Rice Krispies

Grease a small swiss roll tin with a little butter. Break the toffee
into small pieces and put into a large saucepan with the butter and
marshmallows. Melt very slowly over a low heat, stirring all the time.
This will take about 10 minutes. When everything has melted and is
blended together, take off the heat and stir in the Rice Krispies.
Carefully spoon the mixture into the tin and press it down gently
with the back of a metal spoon. Leave to set for 1 hour, then cut
up into squares or rectangles.

NOTE You could even spread melted white or milk chocolate over the
top of this and let it set before you cut it.

NOTE You can also spoon this into paper cases in bun tins, like the
White or Milk Chocolate Chewy Rice Krispie Buns on page 191.

  Children's Birthday Party

Chocolate Brownies

Makes about 16 large or 25 small ones

These are good enough to serve at the end of a dinner party; serve with softly whipped cream and a cup of good coffee. Children will adore them.

180 g (6 oz) butter
180 g (6 oz) good dark chocolate
3 eggs
250 g (9 oz) caster sugar
110 g (4 oz) plain flour
100–150 g (3½–5½ oz) chopped walnuts or muesli (optional)

Preheat the oven to 180°C/350°F/gas 4. Line the bottom of a 20 cm (8 in) square tin or a small (23 x 33 cm /9 x 13 in) swiss roll tin lined with greaseproof paper or tin foil. Carefully melt the butter and chocolate in a pan on a low heat. In a separate bowl, beat the eggs and sugar. When the chocolate has melted, let it cool for a minute and then mix it with the eggs and sugar in the bowl. Stir in the flour and nuts, if using, and beat to combine. Empty into the prepared tin and place in the oven and cook for 32–42 minutes (this depends on the oven). When cooked it should be crisp on top but still slightly dense and fudgy inside. Cut into squares, and when it has cooled take out of the tin.

Homemade Lemonade

Makes 2 litres (3½ pt)

Your little darlings will be a lot less hyper and will have much less of a sugar hangover if you can give them something to drink other than fizzy drinks. This is delicious, but you could also try the Raspberry Lemonade on page 57.

250 g (9 oz) sugar
225 ml (8 fl oz) water
4 lemons, juiced
2 oranges, juiced
1½ litre (2¾ pt) water

To make the syrup, put the sugar in a saucepan with the water on the heat. Slowly bring to the boil, stirring to dissolve the sugar, then boil for 2 minutes and let cool.

Meanwhile, juice the fruit, top up with nearly all the cold sugar syrup, add water to taste and more syrup if it needs it. Put into a jug with ice and serve.

Index

Index